'Anyone who gives so much as a cup of cold water.'

(Matthew 10:42)

In celebration of my twentieth anniversary to the permanent diaconate, within the Catholic Church, I would like to dedicate this book to the people, parish, and school of Our Lady of the Wayside.

I must also dedicate this book to Our Lord and Saviour, Jesus Christ, his people, and his church because as he constantly reminded me throughout the whole writing project, *'for without me you can do nothing.'*

All profits from the sale of this book are being donated to support children at Our Lady of the Wayside Roman Catholic Primary School.

You can find out more about the school and the parish of Our Lady of the Wayside by going to:

www.ol-wayside.solihull.sch.uk

www.ourladyofthewaysidechurchshirley.co.uk

Sean Loone

A Cup of Cold Water

Finding Christ in the Sunday Gospels of Lent and Easter

This edition first published in paperback by
Michael Terence Publishing in 2024
www.mtp.agency

ISBN 9781800946644

Foreword

Whenever I write a book, I never want it to be about me. Rather, it is meant to be about God and his people. If, in some small way, my years of study, prayer and reflection can help others deepen their relationship with God, that will always be enough for me. Yet, and without being self-indulgent, I thought it appropriate, this time, just to add a personal note in the foreword, to this my final book, on the Bible. It was on the 23rd of May 2004 that I was ordained to the permanent diaconate, at Our Lady of the Wayside, Shirley. A parish I have now served for the last twenty years. Hence, as this book will be published in 2024, I felt it appropriate to mark the occasion.

Looking back now, I never would have thought it possible, to have written several books, whilst balancing a pastoral, sacramental and academic ministry, with being a husband and a father. Yet, God's grace, always seems to find a way. The day of my ordination will always stand out for me as one of the highlights of my life as it took place in my home parish, and the one in which I was invited to serve God and his people. It seemed, perfectly right therefore, in this special year, to dedicate this book to the people, and parish of Our Lady of the Wayside. The one thing I have learned, over the years, is that God is often to be found in the place you least expect to see him, but he is always to be found wherever people are. By immersing yourself in people's lives, the scriptures actually come alive, and you find yourself learning more than you teach, about God.

This book, fundamentally, is an attempt to bridge the gap between academic, and biblical theology on the one hand, with the reality of people's lives on the other. I do hope this comes across when you read it. I have made every effort to make it both readable, and accessible to anyone who might find it of interest. Hence, you do not need any knowledge of the Bible, and I have excluded all references and footnotes, in an attempt to avoid any sense of intimidation. I have, though, included all the Bible passages you will need as an immediate companion to the reflections. My hope, though, is that it will enthuse the reader to want to find out more about God's word.

Following on from the style of my last book, I have included a series of questions after each reflection. These are designed, quite rightly, in my opinion, to challenge the reader or the group, to stay with the text, constantly searching, and looking for more. Each reflection is designed to break open the word, but I will be the first to admit, that I do not know all of the answers.

Perhaps, it is best to see this book as a journey through the most sacred, and holy seasons in the church's year, culminating in the resurrection, ascension, and out pouring of the Holy Spirit at Pentecost. Each reflection then acts like a journal accompanying you along the way. Yet, it is God, and God alone who will lead you by and through the grace of his Holy Spirit because it is to him that all glory and praise is due. Having said that, there is also something of myself, inevitably, in each of the reflections. So, in that sense I will also be your travelling companion. When the time comes, on that first Ash Wednesday, let us step out onto the road together, and just like Bilbo Baggins in the Hobbit or Frodo in The Lord of the Rings, begin the biggest adventure of our lives.

God Bless.

Deacon Sean

January 2024

Contents

Introduction

'Anyone who gives so much as a cup of cold water.'

(Matthew 10:42)

Dear Friends

Let me start off by saying a word or two about the title I have chosen for this, my final book, about sacred scripture. Everything I have ever written on the Bible is designed to draw people into an ever-deeper relationship with Christ. One of things which has kept me going, over the years, is the belief that someone, somewhere, might somehow, be helped by the words I have committed to paper. Writing, as you can imagine, can be a lonely enterprise whereby you spend long periods of time, in a room, alone with only a keyboard for company. Yet, this is only part of the story because, for me at least, there is always the presence of the Lord, and his Word, as a constant source of inspiration.

With all this in mind I very often discover that Grace operates as God wills it. I can be reading a piece of scripture, which I have spent time with many times before, when suddenly something new strikes me. This is what happened when I was reflecting on a title for this book. Nothing seemed to come to mind. So, I left it, and then one day, quite literally out of the blue, as I was reading the Gospel of Matthew the title sprang out at me, *'One Cup of cold Water'*. Matthew, in fact, puts it like this, *'Anyone who gives so much as cup of cold water to one of these little ones…'* (Matthew 10:42) Indeed, this is exactly why I write, in the hope that, even if it is only one person who reads it, and in so doing their relationship with Christ is deepened, that would be enough. Hence, it is like giving a cup of cold water to someone who thirsts. Now who would have thought that! It would seem that God does indeed move in mysterious ways.

In this book you will find a series of reflections which will take the reader on a journey through Lent and Easter. Sunday by

Sunday you will be invited to read a passage from the relevant Gospel and spend time simply finding Christ there. At the end of each reflection, you will find a series of questions, which you are invited to answer, in part or in full, as you see fit. Having said that, feel free to ignore them if you wish. For this reason, the process also lends itself to study groups whereby people can share their reaction to the text with each other. Indeed, you might even find yourself disagreeing with my reflection, and that is fine too.

My primary motivation is to brake open the word of God for people today so that they can see its relevancy for their own daily lives. Lecturing at a seminary has taught me the important lesson of helping students, in formation for ministry, to bridge the gap between academic theology and peoples' everyday experiences. It seems to me that the disciples of Jesus were constantly guided by his Word as we should be too. For this reason, the key word for me in making your way through this book is compassion. I would go so far as to say that the first quality of love is compassion, and it is in living lives of compassion that the Kingdom of God is made a reality in the here and now. This was the very essence of the ministry of Jesus, and it is the central theme of this book. Jesus is nothing less than the human face of God, and he invites us to reflect his radical, and compassionate nature, in our discipleship today.

In the life of Jesus, we see God's response to suffering humanity and our journey through Lent and Easter exposes the depth and nature of his outrageous and uncompromising love. Hence, I often make the point, that personal growth in faith, often comes in what appears to the world, as failure. In the same way, true self-knowledge, is born out of the mistakes that we make. Ultimately, God simply invites us to be good, and to live lives which reflect something of his goodness. We may stumble and fall along the way the way, but we can be sure of one thing, that he will always be there with us.

So, I would invite you, to work your way slowly through this book. Ideally, read the text on the appropriate Sunday and stay with it throughout the course of the week, constantly reflecting on its meaning and how it applies to your life of faith. If you are part of a group, be bold enough and strong enough to say what you think, after all what is the worse that could happen? I do hope that you find what I have written useful, and helpful in your own journey of faith. The book is the end product of much study, prayer, and reflection. I am often asked if I write my homilies down, and my answer is always, no. This book, however, is the closest I have ever come, in committing what I have said in church for God's people, to paper. Hence, I offer it in all humility, and as an expression of my own faith, to God, his people, and the advancement of his Kingdom.

God Bless.

Deacon Sean

Year A: Matthew

Matthew and Lent

'One does not live by bread alone,
but by every word that comes from the mouth of God.'
(Matthew 4:4)

One:

Dealing with Temptation

Matthew 4:1-11

First Sunday of Lent

Then Jesus was led up by the Spirit into the wilderness to be tempted by the devil. He fasted forty days and forty nights, and afterwards he was famished. The tempter came and said to him, "If you are the Son of God, command these stones to become loaves of bread." But he answered, "It is written,

'One does not live by bread alone,
but by every word that comes from the mouth of God.'"

Then the devil took him to the holy city and placed him on the pinnacle of the temple, saying to him, "If you are the Son of God, throw yourself down; for it is written,

'He will command his angels concerning you,'
and 'On their hands they will bear you up,
so that you will not dash your foot against a stone.'"

Jesus said to him, "Again it is written,
'Do not put the Lord your God to the test.'"

Again, the devil took him to a very high mountain and showed him all the kingdoms of the world and their splendour; and he said to him, "All these I will give you, if you will fall down and worship me." Jesus said to him, "Away with you, Satan! for it is written,

'Worship the Lord your God,
and serve only him.'"

Then the devil left him, and suddenly angels came and waited on him.

We begin our journey through Lent in the desert. Jesus has fasted for forty days and is hungry and exhausted. His greatest desire is to discern his Father's will. Satan, of course, knows this and seeks to divert Jesus's attention away from God and to himself.

First Temptation – 'If you are the Son of God, tell these stones to become bread'

If we go back to the text the first thing to notice is that Jesus is led into the desert by the Spirit of God. This same Spirit now dwells within him, and it is to this Spirit which he now turns, in resisting all that Satan will throw at him. *'Man does not live on bread alone, but on every word that comes from the mouth of God.'* Here Jesus rejects prioritising his own needs and exhorting himself. This is not who he is called to be. Rather, Jesus will feed the hungry and be sustained by God's living word. There is a powerful message here for those who would follow Jesus today. Hence, the church and all those who would walk in the footsteps of Christ should never put their own interests above that of God's. To do so would make us unfaithful. Indeed, for the church to seek personal gain above that of the poor is to betray the Gospel of Jesus Christ.

Second Temptation – 'If you are the Son of God, throw yourself down'

Now we find Jesus on top of the temple with Satan. Here he is tempted to glorify himself, whilst knowing that God, his Father, will not allow him to be harmed. Jesus, once again, inspired by the Spirit, responds by saying, *'Do not put the Lord your God to the test.'* Jesus refuses to glorify himself. He will not be the Messiah the world expects him to be. No! His mission will not be one which is self-seeking. The glory of his Father will come before his own. In this way, Jesus refuses to perform miracles simply to confirm his identity. Rather he will do the opposite by putting the needs of the despised, rejected, and unwanted, first. As a result, the only signs he will perform will be to bring comfort to the lonely, raise up the fallen, and cure the sick. Once again, we need to be on our guard. The church must never give into the temptation of seeking its own glory at the expense of God's. Rather, its mission should always be to put the needs of others before its own. In this way, the church must always seek the glory of God first. Hence, being faithful to Jesus means living a life of service to all those in need.

Third Temptation – 'Bow down and worship me'

This time we find Jesus at the top of a high mountain from which it is possible to see all the kingdoms of the world. Everything is under the dominion of Satan who now turns to Jesus and makes an unbelievable offer, *'if you bow down and worship me,'* all this will be yours. Jesus's reaction is outright rejection, *'Away from me, Satan! For it is written: "Worship the Lord your God and serve him only."'* In this way, Jesus is rejecting any form of domination, manipulation, coercion, or control associated with his Father. He is not like the earthly powers, personified by the emperor in Rome. No! Jesus has been sent as a servant. His message from the Father to humanity about the kingdom of heaven is one of love not power. In the same way, the church must also resist any temptation to give in to the desire to seek power, glory, manipulation, or control for itself. Rather, its fundamental identity should always be one of service, motivated by love. To seek self-importance, and glorification, in any form, is to be unfaithful to Jesus.

Something to think about and discuss:

1. *What are your own expectations as we enter the season of Lent?*
2. *Thinking about the first temptation how often are we tempted to put self-interest first? How difficult is it to resist this?*
3. *Is it possible to always put the needs of others before our own?*
4. *Do you think the church has been or is guilty of trying to manipulate or control people? Can you think of any examples of this today?*
5. *Do you think Lent still has an important role to play in the life of Christians? Can you give reasons for your answer?*

Two:

Listening to Jesus

Matthew 17:1-9

Second Sunday of Lent

Six days later, Jesus took with him Peter and James and his brother John and led them up a high mountain, by themselves. And he was transfigured before them, and his face shone like the sun, and his clothes became dazzling white. Suddenly there appeared to them Moses and Elijah, talking with him. Then Peter said to Jesus, "Lord, it is good for us to be here; if you wish, I will make three dwellings here, one for you, one for Moses, and one for Elijah." While he was still speaking, suddenly a bright cloud overshadowed them, and from the cloud a voice said, "This is my Son, the Beloved; with him I am well pleased; listen to him!" When the disciples heard this, they fell to the ground and were overcome by fear. But Jesus came and touched them, saying, "Get up and do not be afraid." And when they looked up, they saw no one except Jesus himself alone.

As they were coming down the mountain, Jesus ordered them, "Tell no one about the vision until after the Son of Man has been raised from the dead."

In this reflection, I want us to focus our attention on listening to Jesus. But are we afraid to do so? You see to achieve this we have to place him at the very heart of our lives, and at the centre of the communities to which we belong. Yet are we afraid to really listen to his voice because of the demands it might make upon us? Ultimately, only by listening to Jesus can his word set us free from all those fears which prevent us from becoming his disciples. During Lent then, let us allow his voice to penetrate our hearts, to the point, that our very lives are completely transformed.

On this Second Sunday of Lent notice, first of all, how we find ourselves, once again, on a mountain. Casting our minds back to last week it was on a mountain that Jesus was tempted to gain earthly glory and power for himself. This time, however, Jesus will reveal to Peter, James, and John, the glory of his resurrection.

At the moment of his transfiguration notice how the face of Jesus shines like the sun. In this way, he reveals the origin of his true glory, which lies with the Father. In rejecting the earthly glory offered to him by Satan, Jesus will reveal that it is through his own suffering and crucifixion that his glorification will be achieved. After this, Moses and Elijah appear standing on either side of Jesus. Notice, however, that their faces do not shine, and they speak only to Jesus and not the disciples. In this way, both the law and the prophets recognise the higher authority of Jesus.

At this stage Peter, not for the first time, makes an error by failing to recognise the unique status of Jesus when he says, *'If you wish, I will put up three shelters – one for you, one for Moses, and one for Elijah.'* In other words, Peter sees the three figures before him as equals – hence they all get the same shelter. The important point to make here is that Jesus is unique and cannot, therefore, be compared to anyone or anything else. Perhaps, it is for this reason, that God the Father, interrupts Peter with the proclamation, *'This is my Son, whom I love; with him I am well pleased.'* In other words, the disciples are staring directly into the face of the risen and glorified Son of God. He is like no other and can be compared to no one. His law is above all others and his teaching comes directly from his Father. It is for this reason that you must, *'Listen to him,'* and him alone.

In response to this, the three disciples throw themselves to the ground, facedown, *'full of terror.'* They are, of course, afraid. Was it because, in reality, they were simply too frightened, *'to listen to Jesus?'* Are we also afraid too? Like them are we too fearful because we live in the knowledge that to listen to his voice and to follow him, will involve taking up the cross and walking the path of humble service? Yet, we need to read on because Jesus knowing their fears, as he knows ours, goes to the disciples and gently lays his hands on them, offering them, and in turn us, words of comfort and consolation, *'Get up, do not be afraid.'*

Perhaps, during Lent, this year, we would do well to listen to the unique words of Jesus, allowing them to penetrate our hearts, and along with the disciples, simply get up and follow him.

Something to think about and discuss:

1. *Why do you think the church always presents us with the Transfiguration on the Second Sunday of Lent?*
2. *Why do you think a mountain is chosen as the scene for the Transfiguration? How might this help us today?*
3. *Why do you think the disciples were so afraid? Are we afraid to really listen to the voice of Jesus?*
4. *What can we learn about Jesus from the Transfiguration?*
5. *How can the Transfiguration help us in our journey of faith today?*

Three:

Thirsting for God

John 4:5-42

Third Sunday of Lent

So, he came to a city of Samaria, called Sychar, near the field that Jacob gave to his son Joseph. Jacob's well was there, and so Jesus, wearied as he was with his journey, sat down beside the well. It was about the sixth hour.

There came a woman of Samaria to draw water. Jesus said to her, "Give me a drink." For his disciples had gone away into the city to buy food. The Samaritan woman said to him, "How is it that you, a Jew, ask a drink of me, a woman of Samaria?" For Jews have no dealings with Samaritans. Jesus answered her, "If you knew the gift of God, and who it is that is saying to you, 'Give me a drink,' you would have asked him, and he would have given you living water." The woman said to him, "Sir, you have nothing to draw with, and the well is deep; where do you get that living water? Are you greater than our father Jacob, who gave us the well, and drank from it himself, and his sons, and his cattle?" Jesus said to her, "Everyone who drinks of this water will thirst again, but whoever drinks of the water that I shall give him will never thirst; the water that I shall give him will become in him a spring of water welling up to eternal life." The woman said to him, "Sir, give me this water, that I may not thirst, nor come here to draw."

Jesus said to her, "Go, call your husband, and come here." The woman answered him, "I have no husband." Jesus said to her, "You are right in saying, 'I have no husband;' for you have had five husbands, and he whom you now have is not your husband; this you said truly." The woman said to him, "Sir, I perceive that you are a prophet. Our fathers worshiped on this mountain; and you say that in Jerusalem is the place where men ought to worship." Jesus said to her, "Woman, believe me, the hour is coming when neither on this mountain nor in Jerusalem will you worship the Father. You worship what you do not know; we worship what we know, for salvation is from the Jews. But the hour is coming, and now is, when the true worshipers will worship the Father in spirit and truth, for such the Father seeks to worship him. God is spirit, and those who worship him must worship in spirit and truth." The woman said to him, "I know that Messiah is coming (he who is called Christ); when he comes, he will show us all things." Jesus said to her, "I who speak to you am he."

Just then his disciples came. They marvelled that he was talking with a woman, but none said, "What do you wish?" or, "Why are you talking with her?" So, the woman left her water jar, and went away into the city, and said to the people, "Come, see a man who told me all that I ever did. Can this be the Christ?" They went out of the city and were coming to him. Meanwhile the disciples besought him, saying, "Rabbi, eat." But he said to them, "I have food to eat of which you do not know." So, the disciples said to one another, "Has anyone brought him food?" Jesus said to them, "My food is to do the will of him who sent me, and to accomplish his work. Do you not say, 'There are yet four months, then comes the harvest'? I tell you, lift up your eyes, and see how the fields are already white for harvest. He who reaps receives wages, and gathers fruit for eternal life, so that sower and reaper may rejoice together. For here the saying holds true, 'One sows, and another reaps.' I sent you to reap that for which you did not labour; others have laboured, and you have entered into their labour." Many Samaritans from that city believed in him because of the woman's testimony, "He told me all that I ever did." So, when the Samaritans came to him, they asked him to stay with them; and he stayed there two days. And many more believed because of his word. They said to the woman, "It is no longer because of your words that we believe, for we have heard for ourselves, and we know that this is indeed the Saviour of the world."

Once again, we find Jesus in the desert. He is tired and thirsty. He has spent so much time walking from place to place proclaiming the kingdom of God. His message is a gospel for all people including everyone and excluding no one. Yet, many have rejected him and, perhaps, he needs to spend some time alone. So, he reaches the small village of Sychar, in the land of Samaria. Looking up into the blazing Sun, he shades his eyes and spots a nearby well, that of Jacob, and wearily sits down.

Not long after a woman arrives seeking water from the well. She is alone and a Samaritan. Her intention is to retrieve water from the well but is caught by surprise when Jesus askes her a question, *'Will you give me a drink?'*

There are several things amiss here. The woman is not a Jew but a Samaritan, and therefore a foreigner to Jesus. Secondly, she is alone in the company of a man something which is culturally unacceptable. Finally, having been married several times she is now with a man to whom she is not married, and therefore an outcast to her people. Recognising all of this the woman is shocked at the attitude of Jesus to her. After all, why would a man of such obvious status, lower himself, to ask for a drink from a woman like her? Every fibre of her being tells her, that this is just plain wrong.

Yet, Jesus is speaking directly to her heart. He is someone in need and turns to the woman for aid. He simply wants her help, some water to quench his thirst. The simple truth is that we all know how Jesus is feeling. At times, in all of our lives, we have been alone and in need of help. Think about it for a moment or two, and just be honest with yourself. Alone through fear, sadness, or illness we crave the help of others. Or putting it another way, we thirst for the kind of human companionship that will bring with it comfort and consolation. When this happens, we are invited to set all our differences to one side, and simply reach out to, and respond, to that cry for help. The woman also appears to be surprised that Jesus does not speak to her as one with authority but instead is gentle and tender. Where is the attitude of superiority that she is used to when a Jew addresses a Samaritan?

There is, in fact, something else going on here that the woman only gradually becomes aware of. Jesus is breaking down the barriers that exists between them and creating something new. He now shares with the woman his great desire when he says, *'If you knew the gift of God and who it is that asks you for a drink.'* Here Jesus is offering himself, out of love, to the woman, as the Messiah, the one she and her people have been waiting for all their lives. Yet, the woman has never experienced unconditional love, and she struggles to understand what Jesus is saying. All she sees is a well, and a strange man, and cannot connect the two.

At this point, Jesus goes on to tell her of the water which he is offering her. Such water will quench her thirst forever and come from the inside. It is life-giving water and will lead to life eternal. As she listens something awakens within her, touching her very soul and desiring that of which Jesus speaks, *'Sir, give me this water.'* The simple truth is that we are that woman to whom Jesus speaks. He breaks down all barriers to come to us, and offers us himself, out of love. The first thing we have to do is recognise our need for him, and that we cannot live without him. Just as we need water to live, such is our need for God. This is our great thirst for Christ, which can only be quenched by his love. To recognise this and accept it, moves us into action. How many people out there are thirsting and seeking that which only God can give? Our role is to seek to break down all barriers, which exist between us, offering those who thirst, the unconditional love of God, revealed through his Son.

Something to think about and discuss:

1. *How does the Gospel reading for today make you feel? Can you give some reasons for your answer?*
2. *Thinking about the woman, can you see any links between her and your own life?*
3. *Identify one part of the reflection which you found most helpful and explain why.*
4. *What can the church learn from this Gospel reading about being alive and active in the world today?*
5. *If you were the woman at the well, what would you ask of Jesus?*

Four:

For the Rejected, Despised, Unwanted and Unloved

John 9:1-41

Fourth Sunday of Lent

As he passed by, he saw a man blind from his birth. And his disciples asked him, "Rabbi, who sinned, this man or his parents, that he was born blind?" Jesus answered, "It was not that this man sinned, or his parents, but that the works of God might be made manifest in him. We must work the works of him who sent me, while it is day; night comes, when no one can work. As long as I am in the world, I am the light of the world." As he said this, he spat on the ground and made clay of the spittle and anointed the man's eyes with the clay, saying to him, "Go, wash in the pool of Siloam" (which means Sent). So, he went and washed and came back seeing. The neighbours and those who had seen him before as a beggar, said, "Is not this the man who used to sit and beg?" Some said, "It is he;" others said, "No, but he is like him." He said, *"I am the man." They said to him, "Then how were your eyes opened?"* He *answered, "The man called Jesus made clay and anointed my eyes and said to me, 'Go to Siloam and wash;' so, I went and washed and received my sight." They said to him, "Where is he?"* He *said, "I do not know."*

They brought to the Pharisees the man who had formerly been blind. Now it was a sabbath day when Jesus made the clay and opened his eyes. The Pharisees again asked him how he had received his sight. And he said to them, "He put clay on my eyes, and I washed, and I see." Some of the Pharisees said, "This man is not from God, for he does not keep the sabbath." But others said, "How can a man who is a sinner do such signs?" There was a division among them. So, they again said to the blind man, "What do you say about him, since he has opened your eyes?" He *said, "He is a prophet."*

The Jews did not believe that he had been blind and had received his sight, until they called the parents of the man who had received his sight, and asked them, "Is this your son, who you say was born blind? How then does he now see?" His parents answered, "We know that this is our son, and that he was born blind; but how he now sees we do not know, nor do we know who opened his eyes. Ask him; he is of age; he will speak for himself." His parents said this because they feared the Jews, for the Jews had already agreed that if anyone should confess him to be Christ, he was to be put out of the synagogue. Therefore, his parents said, "He is of age, ask him."

So, for the second time they called the man who had been blind, and said to him, "Give God the praise; we know that this man is a sinner." He answered, "Whether he is a sinner, I do not know; one thing I know, that though I was blind, now I see." They said to him, "What did he do to you? How did he open your eyes?" He answered them, "I have told you already, and you would not listen. Why do you want to hear it again? Do you too want to become his disciples?" And they reviled him, saying, "You are his disciple, but we are disciples of Moses. We know that God has spoken to Moses, but as for this man, we do not know where he comes from." The man answered, "Why, this is a marvel! You do not know where he comes from, and yet he opened my eyes. We know that God does not listen to sinners, but if anyone is a worshiper of God and does his will, God listens to him. Never since the world began has it been heard that anyone opened the eyes of a man born blind. If this man were not from God, he could do nothing." They answered him, "You were born in utter sin, and would you teach us?" And they cast him out.

Jesus heard that they had cast him out, and having found him he said, "Do you believe in the Son of man?" He answered, "And who is he, sir, that I may believe in him?" Jesus said to him, "You have seen him, and it is he who speaks to you." He said, "Lord, I believe;" and he worshiped him. Jesus said, "For judgment I came into this world, that those who do not see may see, and that those who see may become blind." Some of the Pharisees near him heard this, and they said to him, "Are we also blind?" Jesus said to them, "If you were blind, you would have no guilt; but now that you say, 'We see,' your guilt remains.

Imagine what it must be like to be blind from birth. To be surrounded constantly by total darkness. Such is the man in our Gospel reading for today. He has never known the light and is reduced to begging for help. He has been told by his religious leaders that it is because of his or his parent's sin that he has been punished by God. What can he do? Nothing! He simply accepts his fate and lives in the darkness.

Yet things are about to change. One day Jesus arrives and sees him. John repeatedly tells us that Jesus is the *'light of the world.'* What is the man to do now? Perhaps, he was aware of the ancient scriptures, whereby the prophet Isaiah proclaimed that when the time was right, the Messiah would come, and give sight to the blind.

What follows now is an encounter between Jesus and the man born blind. Mixing mud with his saliva Jesus makes a paste which he applies to the eyes of the blind man, and something remarkable happens. First, though, the man has to do what Jesus tells him to do, which is to wash his eyes. Slowly, a cleansing takes place whereby the man's eyes are opened, and for the first time in his life, he begins to see. Astonished the people ask him, who did to this to you, but the man can only respond with a name, Jesus. Equally, when challenged, the man does not know where Jesus is. The only thing he knows for sure is that it was Jesus who opened his eyes. Now, and again for the first time in his life, the man felt free and able to live his life in a new way. This was the only thing which mattered to him.

Soon, however, the religious leaders track him down and demand answers. Yet, he has few answers to offer them. Perhaps, the man is a prophet, but he must come from God to do such a thing as give sight to a blind man. Unable to control their anger the religious leaders insult him and throw him out of the community of believers.

When we return to Jesus, we find him searching for the man who has been expelled. Here is the true nature of God, the one who comes in search of all those who are rejected, despised, unwanted, and unloved. God never turns his back on anyone because he includes rather than excludes, even when it comes to matters of faith, and religion. So, on finding him Jesus asks a simple question, *'Do you believe in the Son of Man?'* Yet, the man hesitates when it comes to a reply because he simply does not have the knowledge to respond. He does, however, have faith and believes in Jesus, so he responds with a question of his own, *'Who is he, Sir? Tell me so that I may believe in him,'* Looking deep into the man's heart Jesus tells him, *'You have seen him; he is the one speaking with you.'* Finally, the man realises what it all means, and looking deep into the eyes of Jesus simply says, *'Lord, I believe.'*

Although this event took place over 2,000 years ago, in Jerusalem, our faith invites us to see it as a living reality in our own lives today. Whereby, in response to the invitation given to us by Jesus to follow him, all we need to say is, *'Lord I believe.'*

Something to think about and discuss:

1. *Can you think of moments of blindness in your own life when you have refused to see the reality of how God acts?*
2. *Who are the despised, rejected, unwanted, and unloved in the world today and what is our reaction to them?*
3. *Can you think of ways that the church pushes people away by making them feel as if they do not belong?*
4. *The church has been described as, a light to the nations, how is this being fulfilled in the world today?*
5. *How can lives of faith give sight to the blind?*

Five:

The Choice is not between Life and Death but between Life and Life

John 11:1-45

Fifth Sunday of Lent

Now a certain man was ill, Lazarus of Bethany, the village of Mary and her sister Martha. It was Mary who anointed the Lord with ointment and wiped his feet with her hair, whose brother Lazarus was ill. So, the sisters sent to him, saying, "Lord, he whom you love is ill." But when Jesus heard it, he said, "This illness is not unto death; it is for the glory of God, so that the Son of God may be glorified by means of it."

Now Jesus loved Martha and her sister and Lazarus. So, when he heard that he was ill, he stayed two days longer in the place where he was. Then after this he said to the disciples, "Let us go into Judea again." The disciples said to him, "Rabbi, the Jews were but now seeking to stone you, and are you going there again?" Jesus answered, "Are there not twelve hours in the day? If anyone walks in the day, he does not stumble, because he sees the light of this world. But if anyone walks in the night, he stumbles, because the light is not in him." Thus, he spoke, and then he said to them, "Our friend Lazarus has fallen asleep, but I go to awake him out of sleep." The disciples said to him, "Lord, if he has fallen asleep, he will recover." Now Jesus had spoken of his death, but they thought that he meant taking rest in sleep. Then Jesus told them plainly, "Lazarus is dead; and for your sake I am glad that I was not there, so that you may believe. But let us go to him." Thomas, called the Twin, said to his fellow disciples, "Let us also go, that we may die with him."

Now when Jesus came, he found that Lazarus had already been in the tomb four days. Bethany was near Jerusalem, about two miles off, and many of the Jews had come to Martha and Mary to console them concerning their brother. When Martha heard that Jesus was coming, she went and met him, while Mary sat in the house. Martha said to Jesus, "Lord if you had been here, my brother would not have died. And even now I know that whatever you ask from God, God will give you." Jesus said to her, "Your brother will rise again." Martha said to him, "I know that he will rise again in the resurrection at the last day." Jesus said to her, "I am the resurrection and the life; he who believes in me, though he die, yet shall he live, and whoever lives and believes in me shall never die. Do you believe this?" She said to him, "Yes, Lord; I believe that you are the Christ, the Son of God, he who is coming into the world."

When she had said this, she went and called her sister Mary, saying quietly, "The Teacher is here and is calling for you." And when she heard it, she rose quickly and went to him. Now Jesus had not yet come to the village but was still in the place where Martha had met him. When the Jews who were with her in the house, consoling her, saw Mary rise quickly and go out, they followed her, supposing that she was going to the tomb to weep there. Then Mary, when she came where Jesus was and saw him, fell at his feet, saying to him, "Lord, if you had been here, my brother would not have died." When Jesus saw her weeping, and the Jews who came with her also weeping, he was deeply moved in spirit and troubled; and he said, "Where have you laid him?" They said to him, "Lord, come and see." Jesus wept. So, the Jews said, "See how he loved him!" But some of them said, "Could not he who opened the eyes of the blind man have kept this man from dying?"

Then Jesus, deeply moved again, came to the tomb; it was a cave, and a stone lay upon it. Jesus said, "Take away the stone." Martha, the sister of the dead man, said to him, "Lord, by this time there will be an odour, for he has been dead four days." Jesus said to her, "Did I not tell you that if you would believe you would see the glory of God?" So, they took away the stone. And Jesus lifted up his eyes and said, "Father, I thank thee that thou hast heard me. I knew that thou hearest me always, but I have said this on account of the people standing by, that they may believe that thou didst send me." When he had said this, he cried with a loud voice, "Lazarus, come out." The dead man came out, his hands and feet bound with bandages, and his face wrapped with a cloth. Jesus said to them, "Unbind him, and let him go."

When someone we love dies our heart breaks. In such moments there is nothing we can do. We do not hear words of consolation as they cannot fill the void. Instead, we tinker on the edge of despair and hopelessness. Yet, in today's Gospel reading, Jesus speaks directly to us, and his words are infused with life. The mistake we make, is in seeing the resurrection of Lazarus as a past event, instead of one which continually takes place here and now.

For the truth is, that God pours his life into our loved ones, because he is the God of the living, not the dead.

The first thing to notice in today's Gospel reading is that Jesus weeps when he hears that his good friend Lazarus has died. Indeed, he has been dead for four days now, his body laid in a tomb blocked by a stone. Sometimes, our faith can be like that – blocked by a stone, unable to see over or around it. When someone whom we love dies we feel completely cut off from them, and alone. All we can do is wait. Wait and hope, that sometime in the future, we will see them again. Our hope, therefore, lies in what, one day, our faith tells us, will be.

With this in mind Martha, along with her sister Mary, rushes out to greet Jesus, expressing her faith in a future resurrection, *'I know that my brother will rise again in the resurrection on the last day.'* Yet, for Jesus, this is not enough. Instead, he offers a simple instruction, *'Take away the stone.'* Marth's reaction is to remonstrate with Jesus, arguing that her brother has been dead for four days, and that by now, his body will have begun to decompose. Jesus simply asks her to believe in him by reassuring her, *'If you believe, you will see the glory of God.'* In other words, if you have faith, you will see how God will give life to your brother.

Once the stone is rolled away, Jesus raises his eyes to heaven, and invites all those who are suffering the crushing blow of bereavement to do the same. All that is required now is faith. So, Jesus thanks his Father, for always listening to him, as he does to us. By now he has stopped crying and is aware that all eyes are on him. He is the way, the truth and the life, and desires that all those present believe he has been sent by the Father. His mission is to bring hope where despair reigns.

In a loud and powerful voice Jesus issues a command, *'Lazarus, come forth.'* What follows now is nothing short of shocking. Out of the dark, dusty tomb, staggers Lazarus bound in his burial shroud, his face wrapped in a cloth. He should be dead, and shows all the signs of death, but he is alive.

Now we can go back to where we started this reflection with all those, we have loved, who have died. To believe in Jesus, is to be believe that he is the God of the living not of the dead. He will never abandon those whom we love to oblivion but rather infuses them with his own life. Faith in Jesus, enables us, to roll the stone away for ourselves, in the sure and certain knowledge that those whom we love and have died are, in fact, alive. When we proclaim this, and bear witness to it, then the resurrection lives in us too.

Something to think about and discuss:

1. *Why do you think this is the last sign performed by Jesus in the Gospel of John?*
2. *Can you explain why today's Gospel reading is often used at funerals?*
3. *What do you find most consoling about what Jesus says in today's Gospel?*
4. *Can you explain the title given to today's reflection?*
5. *How does the Gospel reading for today, awaken our faith in the resurrection, as a lived reality now?*

Six:

Following Jesus

Matthew 26:14-27

Passion (Palm) Sunday

Then one of the twelve, who was called Judas Iscariot, went to the chief priests, and said, "What will you give me if I deliver him to you?" And they paid him thirty pieces of silver. And from that moment he sought an opportunity to betray him.

Now on the first day of Unleavened Bread the disciples came to Jesus, saying, "Where will you have us prepare for you to eat the Passover?" He said, "Go into the city to such a one, and say to him, 'The Teacher says, My time is at hand; I will keep the Passover at your house with my disciples.'" And the disciples did as Jesus had directed them, and they prepared the Passover.

When it was evening, he sat at table with the twelve disciples; and as they were eating, he said, "Truly, I say to you, one of you will betray me." And they were very sorrowful, and began to say to him one after another, "Is it I, Lord?" He answered, "He who has dipped his hand in the dish with me, will betray me. The Son of man goes as it is written of him, but woe to that man by whom the Son of man is betrayed! It would have been better for that man if he had not been born." Judas, who betrayed him, said, "Is it I, Master?" He said to him, "You have said so."

Now as they were eating, Jesus took bread, and blessed, and broke it, and gave it to the disciples and said, "Take, eat; this is my body." And he took a cup, and when he had given thanks he gave it to them, saying, "Drink of it, all of you."

What does it take to be a follower of Jesus? Can there be any half-measures or is it all or nothing? As we reach Passion Sunday this is a demanding question but one, we must ask of ourselves. The truth is, that Jesus makes it very clear what it means, to accept the invitation, to be one of his disciples, when he says, *'If someone wants to come after me, let them take up their cross and follow me.'* But what does that mean, and are we prepared to do it? Yet, we cannot compromise what Jesus is asking of us. To follow him, means to walk his path, and this will, inevitably, involve suffering. Indeed, suffering and discipleship go hand in hand. Hence, the authentic nature of our discipleship will be reflected in our suffering, and there can be no escape from this.

This means that to follow Jesus does demand our all. Yet, what does this mean in our world of today? First of all, it is something real and tangible, and must be reflected, practically, in the way in which we live. It begins with recognising that God's justice must reign in our hearts and be reflected in our day to day lives. To this end, the key word must be compassion, something which Jesus constantly lived out during his earthly life. Secondly, not only must we do this as individuals but as members of communities dedicated to realising the kingdom of God here and now.

What then should such lives and communities look like? In communion with Christ our aim is to conform our lives to that of his. This is achieved by standing up for the truth when we find ourselves confronted by lies and deceit. It means working for justice and peace where we find injustice, cruelty, and violence. It involves, living lives motivated by compassion, bringing love and kindness to all those who suffer. Finally, it means challenging individuals, structures, and systems which in the face of human suffering respond only with indifference. Yet all of this, must be a reflection of what Jesus himself, lived and taught.

Such change does not take place overnight, but it must begin somewhere, and that is with our own hearts. Lives transformed by grace must be reflected in action, but we must accept that this will inevitably involve both conflict and suffering. Any attempt to build a more just world based on the Gospel of Jesus Christ will be met with resistance. This is because many people fear that they will lose that which they have. Once again, we turn to the fate of Jesus, and see what happened to him. Yet his fate, must be ours too, as this is what discipleship actually means. Standing up for the weak, voiceless, and vulnerable conforms our lives to that of Jesus, and attempts to make the world more human.

On this Passion Sunday, we need to give ourselves time, to reflect on what it really means to follow Jesus. We know that there is a price to be paid, but accepting the invitation to walk in his footsteps, will also define who we are as human beings. Yet, can there be anything more important to do in life? To conform our lives, and the communities to which we belong, to the Gospel of Jesus Christ, is to engage with the world, and to challenge its values. If a more a more just world is ever to be achieved, however, it will not be easy, and once again, we return to the words of Jesus himself, *'If someone wants to come after me, let them take up their cross and follow me.'* Now, what are we prepared to do?

Something to think about and discuss:

1. *What does discipleship mean to you?*
2. *What do you think Jesus meant by, 'If someone wants to come after me, let them take up their cross and follow me?'*
3. *What do you think should be the priorities of the church in the world today?*
4. *Based on your own experiences, in what ways does discipleship involve suffering?*
5. *When was the last time you stood up for truth, justice, or compassion?*

Matthew and Easter

'They have taken the Lord out of the tomb,
and we do not know where they have laid him.'
(John 20:2)

Seven:

The Crucified and Risen Lord

John 20:1-9

Easter Sunday

Now on the first day of the week Mary Magdalene came to the tomb early, while it was still dark, and saw that the stone had been taken away from the tomb. So, she ran, and went to Simon Peter and the other disciple, the one whom Jesus loved, and said to them, "They have taken the Lord out of the tomb, and we do not know where they have laid him." Peter then came out with the other disciple, and they went toward the tomb. They both ran, but the other disciple outran Peter and reached the tomb first; and stooping to look in, he saw the linen cloths lying there, but he did not go in. Then Simon Peter came, following him, and went into the tomb; he saw the linen cloths lying, and the napkin, which had been on his head, not lying with the linen cloths but rolled up in a place by itself. Then the other disciple, who reached the tomb first, also went in, and he saw and believed; for as yet they did not know the scripture, that he must rise from the dead.

In our last reflection we spent time thinking about what it meant to accept the invitation to follow Jesus. To do so, involved picking up the cross, and living a life which meant speaking out and defying all forms of injustice, cruelty, and oppression. There would, however, be a price to pay, which might well be our own annihilation. Yet, Christ has been there before us. For he is the crucified God. The victim, who in choosing the rejected, despised, unwanted and unloved was himself put to death in the cruellest way imaginable. This though, was not the last word, for that belonged to God. Jesus's life did not end in failure but rather in resurrection.

What then does this mean for us today? First and foremost, God speaks to us through the resurrection of his Son. In answer to an unjust, and cruel world, God raises his Son up and cries to the oppressed, persecuted, marginalised and unwanted, *come to me.* To all those who strive to make the world in which we live more just and humane God cries, *I am with you.* Little wonder then that those early disciples, and followers of Jesus, had little choice other than to preach the resurrection. This is the Gospel we have to embrace too if we are ever going to be authentic witnesses to Jesus.

It is, in fact, because of the resurrection that everything we do has meaning. At times, it is true, we are threatened to be overwhelmed by the scale of the inhumanity we see and experience in the world, but the resurrection tells us not to lose heart, *'for I am with you.'* You see the resurrection is not just a past event, but an ever-present reality in our lives, which we are called to live. We will still experience abuse, cruelty, and rejection but we do not do so alone. Just like Jesus, we will incur wounds, but one day, they will also be transformed. The message is to keep going, journeying with all those who suffer, whilst all the time bearing witness to resurrected and new life. You see our lives have been transformed by his glory, and one day our scars will be healed by his love.

What we are talking about here is faith in the risen Lord, which will sustain, and strengthen us, as we continue to live our lives according to the values of his kingdom. Hence, our witness, when confronted with despair, has to be one of hope. When we come across evil of any kind, our response has to be one of love. We can never be overwhelmed by what the world throws at us because our Lord and saviour has himself, *'overcome the world.'*

Motivated by the love we have for the risen Lord, we accept his invitation to take up our own cross and follow him, knowing that he is with us always, *'even until the end of time.'* Along the way, we will incur wounds of our own, this is inevitable. We will grow weary, suffer pain and loss, and the tears will flow. Yet faith, hope and love will drive us ever forward following in the footsteps of the crucified God. Eventually, when we reach the end of our own road something will be waiting for us, a total sharing in his resurrected life. At that moment, the tears will be wiped from our own eyes. All pain, suffering and mourning will cease. Then we shall see him face to face, our wounds will be healed, and our lives become one with his.

Something to think about and discuss:

1. *What do you think is meant by, 'The crucified God'?*
2. *Can you explain how the resurrection is not just a past event?*
3. *How difficult is it to be an authentic witness to Jesus today?*
4. *How does God speak to us through the resurrection and what is he saying?*
5. *Why is the resurrection of Jesus so important to Christianity?*

Eight:

The Resurrection and Transformed Existence

John 20: 19-31

Second Sunday of Easter

On the evening of that day, the first day of the week, the doors being shut where the disciples were, for fear of the Jews, Jesus came and stood among them and said to them, "Peace be with you." When he had said this, he showed them his hands and his side. Then the disciples were glad when they saw the Lord. Jesus said to them again, "Peace be with you. As the Father has sent me, even so I send you." And when he had said this, he breathed on them, and said to them, "Receive the Holy Spirit. If you forgive the sins of any, they are forgiven; if you retain the sins of any, they are retained."

Now Thomas, one of the twelve, called the Twin, was not with them when Jesus came. So, the other disciples told him, "We have seen the Lord." But he said to them, "Unless I see in his hands the print of the nails and place my finger in the mark of the nails, and place my hand in his side, I will not believe."

Eight days later, his disciples were again in the house, and Thomas was with them. The doors were shut, but Jesus came and stood among them, and said, "Peace be with you." Then he said to Thomas, "Put your finger here, and see my hands; and put out your hand and place it in my side; do not be faithless but believing." Thomas answered him, "My Lord and my God!" Jesus said to him, "Have you believed because you have seen me? Blessed are those who have not seen and yet believe."

Now Jesus did many other signs in the presence of the disciples, which are not written in this book; but these are written that you may believe that Jesus is the Christ, the Son of God, and that believing you may have life in his name.

Why do some people believe in the resurrection of Jesus whilst others do not? Why does our own faith in the resurrection of Jesus, at times, grow cold? Is it possible to answer these questions at all? In fact, we find the answer in today's Gospel reading. Firstly, note how the Gospel reading starts with the disciples of Jesus locked in a room out of fear. Remember they have already been told by Mary Magdalene that Jesus is risen because she has seen, and experienced, the resurrected Lord for herself. Yet, they remain to be convinced, and are instead, ruled by fear. Even the eyewitness of Mary Magdalene does not remove how they feel. In many ways, it could be said, that they have become prisoners of their own fear. It is as if they are both hopeless and helpless. Gone is the commission given to them by Jesus to take the good news to the ends of the earth. Instead, as night falls, their number one priority now appears to be, their own safety and security.

It would seem, therefore, that knowing Jesus is risen from the dead by itself is not enough. We can apply the same principle to anyone who has heard of the resurrection, and even to our own faith, when it grows cold. So, what is missing then? Perhaps, it is the experience of Jesus himself. There are many examples in the Gospels when, after a trauma, the disciples experienced Jesus directly, and in so doing, he restored their faith. Now locked in a room, and afraid, could it be, that this is what was missing? Nothing less than a direct experience of Jesus himself?

Look what happens when Jesus does, in fact, appear to them; they are, '*overjoyed when they saw the Lord.*' Here then, is the key to understanding everything, which is how experiencing Jesus, in our midst, leads to the transformation of our lives. Yet, this does not just apply to our own individual lives but also to the communities to which we belong. Think about it, the disciples were part of a community when they experienced Jesus. He stood in their midst, they experienced him, and were overcome with joy. When we see, and experience Jesus, in the midst of our own communities, we too will be overcome with joy. All too often, we are like the disciples at the start of today's Gospel reading, overcome by fear. When this happens, our hearts shrink, and we become inward looking, concerned only with our own safety and security. As a result, any sense of joy we might have had fades, and we look for certainty elsewhere. The answer is, of course, to look to Christ, and recognise him at the very centre of our lives, and communities. Only then will we experience the joy of the disciples and be able to offer his peace to others.

Unfortunately, we have a tendency to forget the words of Jesus, *'Where two or three are gathered together in my name I am there in their midst.'* In the same way, we push from our memories, the words of Jesus in today's Gospel reading to Thomas, *'Because you have seen me, you believe; blessed are those who have not seen and yet still believe.'* When this happens the flame of our faith dims, and our communities slowly die. The truth, however, is that Jesus is never absent from our lives, in fact he is closer to us than we could ever imagine and loves us more than we could ever know. But the communities to which we belong must reflect this, if not, then we have nothing to offer the world, Hence, the resurrection must live in us, in our lives of faith, and the communities to which we belong. Only then will others see something different, something attractive and something compelling, and that is, of course, the life of Christ, present and alive in our midst.

To this end, the resurrected Christ must find a home in our hearts and simply live there. We must live our lives of faith knowing, and believing, that Jesus is constantly present in everything we say and do. In other words, we must live our lives as people transformed by the resurrection of Jesus. In this way, it is his peace and his love which we can offer to the world because he lives not just in us but in and through the communities to which we belong. This is something Jesus invites us to commit our whole lives to because as we proclaim at Easter, *we are a resurrection people and alleluia is our song.* Now, therefore, is the time to reflect this with lives of joy and peace because in holding such faith, and living such lives, Jesus tells us, we are '*blessed*.'

Something to think about and discuss:

1. *What does the resurrection mean to you?*
2. *Why do you think the disciples were so afraid at the start of today's Gospel reading?*
3. *How does the resurrection of Jesus change or transform our lives here and now?*
4. *Why do you think it is important for the resurrection of Jesus to be a lived experience?*
5. *How would you explain the importance of the resurrection in your life of faith to someone who struggles to believe in it?*

Nine:

Experiencing Jesus

Luke 24:13-35

Third Sunday of Easter

That very day two of them were going to a village named Emmaus, about seven miles from Jerusalem, and talking with each other about all these things that had happened. While they were talking and discussing together, Jesus himself drew near and went with them. But their eyes were kept from recognizing him. And he said to them, "What is this conversation which you are holding with each other as you walk?" And they stood still, looking sad. Then one of them, named Cleopas, answered him, "Are you the only visitor to Jerusalem who does not know the things that have happened there in these days?" And he said to them, "What things?" And they said to him, "Concerning Jesus of Nazareth, who was a prophet mighty in deed and word before God and all the people, and how our chief priests and rulers delivered him up to be condemned to death and crucified him. But we had hoped that he was the one to redeem Israel. Yes, and besides all this, it is now the third day since this happened. Moreover, some women of our company amazed us. They were at the tomb early in the morning and did not find his body; and they came back saying that they had even seen a vision of angels, who said that he was alive. Some of those who were with us went to the tomb and found it just as the women had said, but him they did not see." And he said to them, "O foolish men, and slow of heart to believe all that the prophets have spoken! Was it not necessary that the Christ should suffer these things and enter into his glory?" And beginning with Moses and all the prophets, he interpreted to them in all the scriptures the things concerning himself.

So, they drew near to the village to which they were going. He appeared to be going further, but they constrained him, saying, "Stay with us, for it is toward evening and the day is now far spent." So, he went in to stay with them. When he was at table with them, he took the bread and blessed, and broke it, and gave it to them. And their eyes were opened, and they recognized him; and he vanished out of their sight. They said to each other, "Did not our hearts burn within us while he talked to us on the road, while he opened to us the scriptures?" And they rose that same hour and returned to Jerusalem; and they found the eleven gathered together and those who were with them, who said, "The Lord has risen indeed, and has appeared to Simon!" Then they told what had happened on the road, and how he was known to them in the breaking of the bread.

In our last reflection we emphasised the importance of how experiencing the resurrection of Jesus can lead to a fundamental change in our lives, which we called, transformed existence. Today, we will explore, how it is possible, to have a lived experience of Jesus, in our lives now.

The Gospel reading often called, *'The Road to Emmaus,'* presents us with a problem, which we also share in today. In so far as, unlike the disciples of Jesus, Mary, and Mary Magdalene, we have no direct experience of an encounter, directly, with Jesus after his death and resurrection. What therefore can we draw upon to help us in our desire to experience the resurrected Christ? The answer actually lies with two disciples of Jesus as they made their way to a place called Emmaus.

The first point to note, is how down they are. In fact, you could go as far as to say, that they had lost their faith in Jesus. Indeed, they appear to question everything they had ever believed in about him even to the point of doubting the resurrection. It is at this point that Jesus joins them in their journey but as Luke tells us, *'Their eyes were unable to recognise him.'* How many people are in exactly the same position today, and how often do we, in all honesty, feel just like that?

Yet, amongst all this apparent doom and gloom there is, in fact, hope. Note, how they continue to talk with enthusiasm about him, calling to mind both his words and deeds. At the same time, the stranger who has joined them, begins to explain the meaning of the scriptures and how it was necessary for the Messiah to suffer and die. Soon a change begins to take place in the disciples as we are told, *'Their hearts begin to burn.'* Here then is the first key to experiencing Jesus in our own lives of faith today, the scriptures. Think of it like this. Our starting point is simply with remembering and talking about Jesus. Stop for a moment and ask yourself the question, *when was the last time you honestly had a conversation with anyone about Jesus?* See what I mean? Hence, our own lives and the communities to which we belong must be places where we can talk about, and reflect upon, the life of Jesus, his message, his deeds, his life, and his death. When we do that, we may well find, a thirst for more, which can, of course, be found in the scriptures. Now, moved by God's grace, we may also find our own hearts, literally, '*burning*' within us as our faith comes alive.

Yet it would seem, based on today's Gospel reading, that the scriptures by themselves are not enough, something more is needed. Luke tells us directly that this is the Eucharist. As they travel on with Jesus the two disciples, still not recognising him, are drawn to this stranger. They have been moved by his words and want to know more. For this reason, as they prepare to stop, they implore him to stay with them. Here, we are seeing, the disciples expressing a need, which is simply to be in the presence of Jesus, '*stay with us,*' they say and, of course, he does.

Then something quite remarkable happens, '*When he was at table with them, he took bread, gave thanks, broke it, and gave it to them. Then their eyes were opened, and they recognised him.*' In that moment, and finally, the two disciples recognised the stranger in their midst as Jesus, '*their eyes were opened,*' and they rushed back to Jerusalem to tell their brothers of the good news.

There are, therefore, two key experiences to be found in today's Gospel reading which are also open to us. The first, is to immerse ourselves in the message of Jesus, found in the scriptures, and to talk about what this means to us often. By reading about, reflecting upon, and sharing his message our hearts too, will *burn within us.* Secondly, by sharing in the Eucharist, we will be touched by his presence whereby, as an act of love, he reaches out to, and feeds, comforts, and strengthens us. When these two strands of faith meet, and penetrate our hearts, we directly experience the presence of the risen Jesus in our lives today. On discovering this, the two disciples, on the road to Emmaus, rushed directly back to

Jerusalem, to share their good news with the disciples. I wonder what we will do.

Something to think about and discuss:

1. *How important is reading and discovering Jesus in the scriptures to you?*
2. *Why do you think the disciples were unable to recognise Jesus in today's Gospel reading?*
3. *When was the last time your heart burned within you as a result of experiencing Jesus?*
4. *What can be done to reawaken, within us, an enthusiasm for the scriptures?*
5. *What does to participate in the celebration of the Eucharist mean to you? Try to give reasons for your answer.*

Ten:

Who Am I?

John 10:1-10

Fourth Sunday of Easter

"Very truly, I tell you, anyone who does not enter the sheepfold by the gate but climbs in by another way is a thief and a bandit. The one who enters by the gate is the shepherd of the sheep. The gatekeeper opens the gate for him, and the sheep hear his voice. He calls his own sheep by name and leads them out. When he has brought out all his own, he goes ahead of them, and the sheep follow him because they know his voice. They will not follow a stranger, but they will run from him because they do not know the voice of strangers." Jesus used this figure of speech with them, but they did not understand what he was saying to them."

So again, Jesus said to them, "Very truly, I tell you, I am the gate for the sheep. All who came before me are thieves and bandits; but the sheep did not listen to them. I am the gate. Whoever enters by me will be saved and will come in and go out and find pasture. The thief comes only to steal and kill and destroy. I came that they may have life and have it abundantly."

Let us begin this reflection by calling to mind some of the titles Jesus applies to himself in the Gospel of John:

'I am the bread of life'

'I am the light of the world'

'I am the good shepherd'

Now let us think about what this means for us, and our lives of faith today. Here we need to keep in mind that only Jesus can fulfil our deepest needs, and desires, because:

The food given to us by Jesus means that we will never be hungry

The light offered to us by Jesus means that we will never walk in darkness

The voice of Jesus spoken to us means that we will be led to the fulness of life

Yet, in today's Gospel reading, we come across another way in which Jesus leads us to a deeper understanding of what following him actually means. Here he uses the image of a door by simply saying, *'I am the door.'* In saying this, Jesus is offering us an invitation to find him through a door which is always open. If we accept that invitation, we will find ourselves in a place we could have never imagined. Yet, it will yield the answer to the question, '*Who am I?*' Because our way of understanding, and living life, will be completely transformed.

John then sets about explaining how this will be achieved in three ways:

1. *'Whoever enters through me will be saved.'* Life, of course, is full of choices. Every day we make them, some being good, whilst others are simply bad. Some will make us more human whilst others will, in effect, dehumanise us. Here Jesus offers a simple invitation to follow him, and in so doing, discover not only who we are but the fullness of life itself. Ultimately, the decision to follow Jesus will lead to a new understanding of the way in which life is to be truly lived.

2. *'They will come in and go out.'* Here the emphasis is on freedom. Anyone who chooses, of their own free will, to follow Jesus is never forced to do so. Jesus is not about coercion, manipulation, or control. Rather, he is about love. Hence, the person who commits themselves to him need not fear anything, including walking away. That is because, the door back, always remains open, and the spirit of his grace is given as a free gift. So, Jesus tells us openly, and plainly, that we can come and go as we please, but always, passing through him.

3. *'And find pasture.'* Here, Jesus tells us that those who enter the door will *find pasture,* which means that both hunger and thirst will cease to exist. God will provide all that is needed to thrive. We will, literally, want for nothing because our deepest needs, and desires, will be met by him.

In this Gospel reading Jesus is, once again, inviting us to come back to him. Only Jesus, therefore, can help us discover who we really are. Yet, to achieve this, we must re-establish our relationship with him. How though, is this to be done, practically in the world today? Here are some obvious suggestions:

- Return to, and learn to love the scriptures – spending periods of time reflecting on what Jesus is saying to us through his word
- Develop a life of prayer – here just be open and honest, talking to God like you would to a good friend or relative
- Rediscover the sacraments – join a worshipping church community, and put down some firm roots
- Conform your life to that of Christ though acts of kindness, love, and charity
- Spiritual reading – find a book or author you like and simply enjoy the journey

The simple truth, which we learn from today's Gospel reading, is that only Jesus can lead us to a new understanding, and appreciation, of who we really are. That only by following in his footsteps and entering the door, which is Christ, can the fullness of life ever be achieved. Ultimately, by immersing ourselves totally in Jesus, we will discover who we really are, as people loved unconditionally by God. When that happens, we will be truly free to be the person we were always destined to be. This is because, in learning who God is, we find out, who we are.

Something to think about and discuss:

1. *How would you answer the question, 'Who am I?'*
2. *Write down a list of the 'I am' sayings from John's Gospel. There should be seven. What do they tell us about Jesus?*
3. *Why do you think Jesus said, 'They will come in and go out?' When referring to himself as the door?*
4. *What do you do, to continuously develop your relationship with Jesus? What do you find most useful and why?*
5. *What would you like your parish to do to help people develop a closer relationship with Jesus? What are you prepared to do to make this possible?*

Eleven:

The Way Home

John 14:1-12

Fifth Sunday of Easter

"Do not let your hearts be troubled. Believe in God, believe also in me. In my Father's house there are many dwelling places. If it were not so, would I have told you that I go to prepare a place for you? And if I go and prepare a place for you, I will come again and will take you to myself, so that where I am, there you may be also. And you know the way to the place where I am going." Thomas said to him, "Lord, we do not know where you are going. How can we know the way?" Jesus said to him, "I am the way, and the truth, and the life. No one comes to the Father except through me. If you know me, you will know my Father also. From now on you do know him and have seen him."

Philip said to him, "Lord, show us the Father, and we will be satisfied." Jesus said to him, "Have I been with you all this time, Philip, and you still do not know me? Whoever has seen me has seen the Father. How can you say, 'Show us the Father'? Do you not believe that I am in the Father and the Father is in me? The words that I say to you I do not speak on my own; but the Father who dwells in me does his works. Believe me that I am in the Father and the Father is in me; but if you do not, then believe me because of the works themselves. Very truly, I tell you, the one who believes in me will also do the works that I do and, in fact, will do greater works than these, because I am going to the Father.

Today's Gospel reading is, very often, the one used most at funerals. In this reflection, we will discover why that is.

The first thing for us to think about is separation. When someone we love dies, we are physically separated from them, and it breaks our heart. In the Gospel reading the disciples discover that they too are to be separated from Jesus. Knowing this he comforts them with these words, *'Do not let your hearts be troubled. Trust in God; trust also in me.'* These are the words offered by Jesus to all those who mourn.

Yet, there is more to come, both for the disciples and in turn us, and for all those whose hearts are broken by the death of a loved one. This is because Jesus is going to say now the like of which has never been said before, and his words should make the hairs on the back of our necks stand up, *'I am going to prepare a place for you in the house of my Father.'* Here Jesus is telling us that death is not the end. No! Rather, in death, life is changed or transformed. The love we have for each other cannot be destroyed by death, and one day, we will be reunited again. After this, Jesus confuses the disciples when he says, *'You know the way to the place where I am going.'* Perhaps, ruled by the fear of being separated from Jesus, they now become uncertain, as to what to say in response. Yet, when faced with the utter loss of a loved one, to whom are we to turn and place all our hope?

At this point, on behalf of the disciples, and perhaps all of us too, Thomas asks, *'Lord we don't know where you are going, so how can we know the way?'* In response, we have those marvellous and comforting words of Jesus, *'I am the way the truth and the life. No one comes to the Father except through me.'* In other words, it is by placing all our hope, and all our trust in Jesus that we will be led to the Father. Everything else will lead us away from him but by following Jesus, we will, in turn, find our Father.

However, there is still hesitation amongst the disciples, and all too often we can feel like that too. Belief in God by itself is not enough, it cannot fulfil our deepest desires and longings, something else, something more, is needed. At this point, Jesus is offering his disciples, and in turn us, something completely different, which they, at the time, were struggling to comprehend. Hence, Philip says, *'Lord show us the Father, and that will be enough for us.'*

The response of Jesus to this is, literally, mind-blowing, *'Whoever has seen me, has seen the Father.'* In the life of Jesus, we see clearly visible, and before our very eyes, God. Everything Jesus said and did reveal the nature and being of his Father. His mercy, compassion, forgiveness and love, his concern and solidarity with the despised, rejected, and unwanted, his desire to heal and make whole, all make the Father present in and through his life. The mystery of the God who is not distant and remote but comes in search of us, simply because he loves us, is to be found wholly, in Jesus.

Yet, there is still even more to come. Once again, let us return to the fear the disciples experienced by the thought of being separated from Jesus, and our own fear when confronted with the death of a loved one. The words Jesus offers seek to console and comfort us, *'I am going to prepare a place for you. And if I go and prepare a place for you, I will come back and take you with me that you may also be where I am.'* Here, we are told, that there is, in fact, nothing to fear, not even death itself. For when that moment comes, and it surely will, to all of us. It is Jesus himself who will return and take us home, so that we can be, where he is. The only question remaining now therefore is, *what do we do in the meantime?* And the answer to this is quite simple. We look to Jesus, and we follow him, so that his way becomes our way too. By living lives of mercy, compassion, forgiveness, and love, by including the excluded, by speaking out on behalf of the voiceless, by being on the side of the rejected, despised, unwanted and unloved, the resurrected Jesus is made clearly visible in us, and our lives of faith. By living lives in the here and now which conform, as far as possible, to that of Jesus, we are giving others a foretaste of what heaven is actually like. Remember that Jesus only gave his disciples, and in turn us, one commandment, which is to love one another in the same way he loves us.

Jesus tells us that we belong to the Father, and our destiny is to be with him forever. True discipleship, therefore, is reflected in how we live with each other, until that day comes. By conforming our lives to that of Jesus, every encounter we have with another person will either give life or drain it. Above all, in the Gospel reading for today, we learn that Christianity is not about what we have done for God but rather, what God has done for us, in and through the life, death, and resurrection of his Son, Jesus Christ.

Something to think about and discuss:

1. *Reflect on your own feelings about death? What happens?*
2. *How does today's reading make you feel when it comes to understanding death and resurrection?*
3. *The reflection describes how Jesus comes to take us home. What do you think is meant by this?*
4. *How would you explain a Christian understanding of death to someone who is afraid of dying?*
5. *How can our lived discipleship now, provide hope to the hopeless, and all those suffering from despair?*

Twelve:

Seeing, Experiencing and Living the Truth

John 14:15-21

Sixth Sunday of Easter

"If you love me, you will keep my commandments. And I will ask the Father, and he will give you another Advocate, to be with you forever. This is the Spirit of truth, whom the world cannot receive, because it neither sees him nor knows him. You know him, because he abides with you, and he will be in you.

"I will not leave you orphaned; I am coming to you. In a little while the world will no longer see me, but you will see me; because I live, you also will live. On that day you will know that I am in my Father, and you in me, and I in you. They who have my commandments and keep them are those who love me; and those who love me will be loved by my Father, and I will love them and reveal myself to them."

Today we begin our reflection with a fundamental question, *'What will the disciples do without Jesus?'* Once Jesus physically leaves the world, he will not be able to be seen. For many, it will be like he never existed. Indeed, although some will seek to prove, with certainty, that a person called Jesus really walked the earth, for most he will become an irrelevance. Yet, for those who look with the eyes of faith, Jesus will be as present as he ever was, in fact, more so. The key to this, however, will be simply to love him, and in return they will be able to experience his life-giving existence.

The most important thing for the Christian is not to associate Jesus, exclusively, with the past. Rather, he must be seen as a present reality. When this happens, we can develop a living relationship with Jesus in the here and now, by loving him unconditionally, in the same way he loves us. This means, we can also begin to see the importance of conforming our lives to that of his. So that his teachings, values, and attitudes are made clearly visible and manifest in us, hence Jesus says, *'If you love me, you will obey what I command.'* As this begins to take shape in our daily lives

John calls it, the *'Spirit of truth.'* Putting it another way, by committing our lives to Jesus his Spirit breaks forth in, and through, our own lives of faith. In this way, we are being led to nothing less than the truth, which must find expression in our lives, no matter where we find ourselves.

Jesus now takes us even deeper into understanding what faith in him really means, *'You are in me, and I am in you.'* We need to spend time with these words pondering on the enormity of what they mean. Jesus also once said, *'I am the light of the world, anyone who believes in me will never walk in darkness,'* and *'no one lights a lamp to put it under the table.'* Faith in Jesus means being his light in the world as he lives in, and through, our lives of faith. There is never a moment or second whereby he is not present in our life. He invites us to listen to him in the depths of our hearts and reflect what we find there by the way in which we live.

Jesus actually tells us, *'Before long, the world will not see me anymore, but you will see me. Because I live you also will live.'* Such comforting, and consoling words, make something very clear, that nothing can ever separate us from the life of Jesus, dwelling in us. This is because his Spirit will be always with us, living within the depths of our hearts. Unlike the physical Jesus nothing and no one can kill or destroy his *Spirit*, hence he will now always be present in the world. For those looking for meaning and purpose in life Jesus makes something abundantly clear, *'I will not leave you as orphans; I will come to you.'* All that we have to do, is to recognise and accept him. To achieve this, search the depths of your own heart and realise that you were never, ever, really alone. That Jesus has always been there waiting for you because he loves you unconditionally and offers his life-giving *Spirit* as a free gift. When that happens, transformation takes place because his life finds expression in ours. On that day everything will change, and nothing will ever be the same again.

Something to think about and discuss:

1. *Why do you think some people believe in Jesus whilst others do not?*
2. *Why do you believe in Jesus, and what impact does this have on how you live your life?*
3. *How would you describe 'The Spirit of Truth' which Jesus tells us we are given by the Father?*
4. *What do you think is meant by, 'Living the Truth?'*
5. *What challenges do you face in living out your faith in the world today?*

Thirteen:

'Go and make disciples'

Matthew 28: 16-20

The Ascension of the Lord

Now the eleven disciples went to Galilee, to the mountain to which Jesus had directed them. When they saw him, they worshiped him; but some doubted. And Jesus came and said to them, "All authority in heaven and on earth has been given to me. Go therefore and make disciples of all nations, baptizing them in the name of the Father and of the Son and of the Holy Spirit, and teaching them to obey everything that I have commanded you. And remember, I am with you always, to the end of the age."

The first thing to note here, is how the disciples made their way to Galilee because this is what Jesus told them to do. Perhaps, Jesus did this because he wanted them to see their former lives, with him, in that place, through the new eyes of the resurrection. Now everything would begin to make sense, as Jesus invited them to continue his mission. Hence, like him, they were to teach the people of the Father, as he did, by using parables. They were, like him, to relieve the pain, misery, and suffering of the broken. They were, like him, to bring God's forgiveness to all those who felt rejected, despised, unwanted, and unloved. And, like him, they were to include everyone and exclude no one.

Yet, *'some doubted,'* even though they worshipped him. Here, Matthew may well be reflecting the fears of early Christian communities as they contemplated a future without Jesus being physically present with them. So, the evangelist, through his Gospel, is attempting, above all things, to inspire trust in Jesus. The danger being, that if this did not happen, all would be lost.

For this reason, Matthew has Jesus approach the disciples, and through the power of his resurrection, makes a declaration of who he is, *'All authority in heaven and on earth has been given to me.'* Jesus is the resurrected one, the Son of God who has received all authority from his Father. All they, and therefore we, need to do now, is place all our hope, and all our trust, in him. It is at this point, that Jesus makes clear what following him, from now on, really means, *'Go and make disciples of all nations.'* On this, everything which they do, will depend. They may well preach, teach, heal, and bear witness, but nothing is more important than making disciples for Jesus.

Hence, there is no escaping the fact, that this is our mission too, simply to make disciples for the Lord. But what does this mean? Here, we are really talking about making disciples for Jesus. For this reason, they and therefore we, must know him, love him, and be his presence in the world. In this task, Jesus will not leave us alone but has promised, *'And surely I am with you always, to the very end of the age.'* Thus, the Gospel, and its message of life in Christ, must be taken to all the nations of the world. Fundamental to the proclamation of the Gospel is baptism, and the passing on of, *'everything I have commanded you.'* In other words, one of the primary missions of the church, is to teach others how to become disciples of Jesus.

A church filled with the spirit of its risen Lord, through which it is strengthened and sustained, will have the faith to confidently teach others how to become authentic witnesses to Christ. Nothing can be more important than this God given task, which is to engage with others in a learning process about what it means to be a disciple of Jesus. With the risen Lord at the heart of our communities of faith, he remains alive and present, energising us with his life-giving spirit. From this we must take courage, knowing and believing that in every Christian community stands the risen Christ continuing to forgive and heal his people. By walking in his footsteps, our mission is to bring others to him, so that, they too, may find the fullness of life. I will, however, leave you with this one final thought for reflection. *Once the Gospel of Jesus Christ captures your heart, you cannot wait to share it with others.*

Something to think about and discuss:

1. *Why do you think Jesus told the disciples to meet him on a mountain in Galilee?*
2. *Why do you think some of the disciples 'still doubted' Jesus?*
3. *How can we, and therefore the church, make disciples of all nations today?*
4. *Is Jesus at the heart of our own lives of faith, and that of the church? How can we tell?*
5. *What can the church do better in preparing the faithful to bring others to Jesus?*

Fourteen:

Wounded Healers

John 20:19-23

Pentecost Sunday

When it was evening on that day, the first day of the week, and the doors of the house where the disciples had met were locked for fear of the Jews, Jesus came and stood among them and said, "Peace be with you." After he said this, he showed them his hands and his side. Then the disciples rejoiced when they saw the Lord. Jesus said to them again, "Peace be with you. As the Father has sent me, so I send you." When he had said this, he breathed on them and said to them, "Receive the Holy Spirit. If you forgive the sins of any, they are forgiven them; if you retain the sins of any, they are retained."

Something wonderful happens in today's Gospel reading if we take the time to read it and allow it to sink into the depths of our soul.

The first thing to note, is how Jesus stands in the midst of his disciples. He does so, as their crucified and risen Lord. Yet, he still carries the wounds of the crucifixion on his body. Thus, there can be no hiding from the fact that those who accept his invitation, to walk in his footsteps, will like him, be wounded.

The next thing to note, is how Jesus offers them his peace in the words, *'Peace be with you.'* This, of course, is a peace the world cannot give. Yet, his wounds are never too far away, when we are told, *'After he said this, he showed them his hands and his side.'*

We now come to why Jesus has called his brothers together, he has a mission for them. Their task now will be nothing less than to make him present in the world. They have had the privilege of experiencing him personally and directly, now they must make this live for others.

At this point in the encounter, Jesus makes clear, what he has in mind for them, *'As the Father has sent me, so I send you.'* In other words, they are to share directly in the mission of Jesus. So, just as

Jesus was in the world, they will be too. Yet, Jesus does not indicate, in fact, what they are to do. This is because they already know, having spent the last few years with him. Nothing less than total commitment to the mission, however, is called for. This can be deduced, plainly, from Jesus showing them his wounds, which from now on, will be their wounds too. Walking in their master's footsteps, they will make him present to a wounded and lost humanity. They will preach, and teach, the mercy and forgiveness of God. They will announce *good news* to the poor. They will heal the sick and include the excluded. They will be the voice for the voiceless and seek out those on the margins. They will incarnate, make flesh, in their own lives, the love and compassion of God for all people. They will seek the way of justice, and peace, even to the point of laying down their own lives. For this is what it means to be a disciple of Jesus.

Yet, Jesus also knows his brothers are weak, and if they are to complete his mission, they will need his help. For this reason, he now does something for them the like of which had not been done since the creation of the world, '*He breathed on them and said, Receive the Holy Spirit.*' When God created Adam and Eve out of the dust of Earth, to give them life, we are told, he breathed on them. In this way, they were given the life-giving Spirit of God, which made them human. It is this same, life-giving Spirit, which Jesus breathed on his disciples, giving them the strength to complete their mission, whilst assuring them of his constant presence. Hence, they would never be alone.

What about us, today, seeking to be disciples of Jesus in the world? The first thing to note, is that just like the disciples, we are also weak, and in need of his life-giving Spirit, for without that we can do nothing. Secondly, we are also wounded because life does that to you. Yet, such wounds are to be transformed by his grace, so that we too, just like the disciples, are to be wounded healers. Hence, the starting point for us is to recognise that without Jesus, and his life-giving Spirit, we can do nothing. So, when others look at us what do they see and experience? Is it the peace and joy that only faith in the risen Christ can bring? Are we the wounded healers, who despite the brokenness of our own lives, can still incarnate, make real and present, his mercy, compassion, forgiveness, and love? Are we committed to the poor, despised, rejected and unwanted? Do we stand up for justice and peace, no matter what the cost? Ultimately, perhaps, there is only one test which clearly demonstrates to the world, whether our lives are fuelled by his life-giving Spirit or not, and it comes directly from Jesus himself. Do we love others in the same way, we know and believe, he loves us? For this, and this alone, is the only thing which matters.

Something to think about and discuss:

1. *Why does Jesus still carry the wounds of the crucifixion on his body after his resurrection from the dead?*
2. *Why do you think the first thing Jesus does, after his resurrection, is offer the disciples his peace?*
3. *How are we weak in our discipleship today?*
4. *What do you think is meant by the term 'wounded healers'?*
5. *Have you any ideas or suggestions as to how the church, today, can revive a sense of mission?*

Year B:
Mark

Mark and Lent

'The time is fulfilled, and the kingdom of God has come near;
repent and believe in the good news.'
(Mark 1:15)

One:

Sent by the Spirit

Mark 1:12-15

First Sunday of Lent

And the Spirit immediately drove him out into the wilderness. He was in the wilderness forty days, tempted by Satan; and he was with the wild beasts; and the angels waited on him.

Now after John was arrested, Jesus came to Galilee, proclaiming the good news of God, and saying, "The time is fulfilled, and the kingdom of God has come near; repent, and believe in the good news."

It is easy to miss, in this short passage that Jesus was actually sent by the Spirit into the desert. It would seem, therefore, that Jesus needed to discover something about himself, and that the best place to do this was the wilderness. Ahead of him Jesus will face many trials, tribulations, and dangers. In the desert, however, he will have the opportunity to spend time, exclusively, with his Father, in silence and prayer. This is something Jesus will need to return to time, and time again, throughout his earthly ministry. The desert, and solitude, was the place people associated with the presence God, ever since their ancestors encountered him there generations before.

Once again, Mark is rather brief when he tells us that Jesus was tempted by Satan because we are told nothing of what this involves. Yet we know that Satan stands in opposition to God and therefore his Son. Hence, his plan is simple, to destroy humanity by defeating and humiliating Jesus. In this way God's plan for the salvation of the world will be reduced to ruins. However, Satan does not make another appearance in Mark. Yet, Jesus identifies him everywhere, especially in those, including Peter, who seek to thwart the mission given to him by his Father.

As we draw to the end of the passage, Mark focuses our attention to two contrasting things: wild animals and angels. Mark does this to make two points. Firstly, the wild animals represent or stand for all the dangers which will constantly threaten Jesus seeking to destroy his plan to save the world from sin. Whilst the angels draw our attention to how close the Father is to the Son, revealing his tenderness and love, and the fact that his mission cannot fail.

Now let us see what happens when we apply this to our own lives, and that of the church today. There can be little doubt, as things stand, that Christianity, at least in the western world, is facing huge challenges. So, what are we to do in response to increasing secularisation and rejection? Perhaps, we need to look to Our Father first, and along with Jesus, accept his invitation to go out into the wilderness. There we can spend time in his presence, and reflect on what we need to do, and what path we must take, if we are ever to rediscover what it means to be an authentic witness to Christ. Where, for example, did we go wrong? In what ways did we fail to stay close to the Lord, and succumb to that which the world offers? At what point, did we lose credibility in the ways in which we lived out our faith? Was it possible, that as a church, we sort power, and control, over the people of God? Did we put self-glory, success, and our own status before the Kingdom of Heaven? Is it possible to stop, reassess our priorities, and take the narrow road back home to the Father who lovingly waits for us to return?

Perhaps, what we need to do more than anything else, is to see the times in which we live as an opportunity; a fresh chance to renew our relationship with the living God. Recall, how the Spirit sent Jesus out into the desert, where there was both wild animals and angels. Today, it seems like we are surrounded by wild animals on all sides but let us not forget the presence of the angels, and therefore the nearness of God. If God sent us here, then it must be for a reason, and something needs to emerge which was better than that which existed before. Hence, we must see the current climate, in which we live, as a time of grace and therefore, not be consumed, and overwhelmed by doom and gloom. For God will not allow his church, which is the body of his Son, to fail. Yet, we must be honest with ourselves, and resist all the temptations which the modern world throws at us, to lead us to away from our saviour. As we start the season of Lent then, let us welcome this holy time, recognising in a positive way that it is God, himself, who sends us out into the wilderness, so that something new can emerge. Something so close to God that the world cannot possibly fail to recognise, the face of his living presence, in us.

Something to think about and discuss:

1. *What do you expect to get from Lent this year?*
2. *What are the main challenges facing the church in the modern world today?*
3. *Why do you think so many people have left the church and what does this say about its witness to the faith?*
4. *In what ways, if any, do you think the church needs to change?*
5. *What does the church mean to you? Describe the positive role the church has in the world of today and for tomorrow.*

Two:

Listen to Jesus

Mark 9:2-10

Second Sunday of Lent

Six days later, Jesus took with him Peter and James and John, and led them up a high mountain apart, by themselves. And he was transfigured before them, and his clothes became dazzling white, such as no one on earth could bleach them. And there appeared to them Elijah with Moses, who were talking with Jesus. Then Peter said to Jesus, "Rabbi, it is good for us to be here; let us make three dwellings, one for you, one for Moses, and one for Elijah." He did not know what to say, for they were terrified. Then a cloud overshadowed them, and from the cloud there came a voice, "This is my Son, the Beloved; listen to him!" Suddenly when they looked around, they saw no one with them anymore, but only Jesus.

As they were coming down the mountain, he ordered them to tell no one about what they had seen, until after the Son of Man had risen from the dead. So, they kept the matter to themselves, questioning what this rising from the dead could mean.

On this Second Sunday of Lent, we are given the Transfiguration to reflect on. So, let us begin with a question, why does Jesus take Peter, James, and John with him? Could it be that Jesus knew how much all three of them failed to comprehend the road he must tread? After all, Peter on more than one occasion, would attempt to dissuade him from his passion. Whilst James and John were, at times, obsessed with attaining the highest places in the Kingdom of Heaven. Could it be therefore, that it was for these reasons that Jesus chose them to witness, first hand, his Transfiguration?

When we come to the actual event there can be little doubt that, in Jesus, the glory of God is fully revealed. At the same time, both Moses and Elijah, representing the Law and the Prophets, were also associated with escaping death and living close to God. With our eyes of faith, today, we are able to see Jesus here as our risen

Lord, the one who was crucified, dead and buried but raised by the Father. Witnessing this spectacular event, it is Peter, true to form, who responds with the words, *'Rabbi, it is good for us to be here. Let us put up three shelters – one for you, one for Moses and one for Elijah.'*

Here we learn two important things about how Peter interprets what he sees. Firstly, he sees all three figures as being equal, hence they will receive a shelter each, as their status is the same. Secondly, he cannot, and will not, see the road ahead for Jesus as one which must lead, inevitably, to his passion and death. Perhaps, it is for this reason, that it is the Father, himself, who will reveal the unique status of Jesus, when he says, *'This is my beloved Son.'* In this way, he cannot, and must not, be compared to anyone else. Yet, this is not enough, because the Father goes on to say, *'Listen to him.'* Ultimately, this will involve, Jesus talking of his passion and death, even then, he must be listened to, because everything will lead to his resurrection.

This is an important lesson we must learn today. Jesus is the source of all truth, and all light radiates from him. In this way, he cannot be compared to anyone else, even Moses, the Law, Elijah, and the Prophets. After all, as Saint John tells us, only Jesus is '*the word made flesh.'* Listening to Jesus, however, as the Father invites us to, will never be easy. In fact, it often comes at great cost. After all, it is Jesus who invites us to take up our cross and follow him. It is Jesus who invites us to join our lives with his, walking the narrow road of faith, whilst facing ridicule and persecution.

Peter's mistake, therefore, must never be ours. Could it be that he equated the Jesus he saw at the Transfiguration with only glory and success? As a result, there was no room in Peter's heart for the passion and crucifixion to come. The truth, however, is that there can be no glory without the pain, suffering and humiliation of the cross. Persecution, opposition, and rejection are the inevitable consequences of becoming a disciple of Jesus Christ. This is what Peter, perhaps, failed to grasp. We must never fall into the trap of equating our faith with the kind of success defined by the world in which we live. Rather, we must grasp the fact, that our true identity, is found in the cross, beyond which lies our ultimate destiny, resurrected glory.

Something to think about and discuss:

1. *What does the Transfiguration of Jesus mean to you?*
2. *Why do you think the Transfiguration is always offered to us, by the church, on the Second Sunday of Lent?*
3. *Why do you think Peter said, what he said, having witnessed the Transfiguration?*
4. *Do you think there is a danger of the church, and Christians, not really listening to what Jesus has to say?*
5. *Spend some time reflecting on the meaning of success when it comes to the living out of Christian discipleship. What conclusions, if any, do you come to?*

Three:

A New Way of Experiencing God

John 2:13-25

Third Sunday of Lent

When the time of the Passover of the Jews was near, Jesus went up to Jerusalem. In the temple he found people selling cattle, sheep, and doves, as well as money changers seated at their tables. Making a whip of cords, he drove them all out of the temple, including the sheep and the cattle. He also overturned the tables of the money changers, scattering their coins, and to those who were selling the doves he ordered, "Take them out of here! Stop turning my Father's house into a marketplace!" His disciples recalled the words of Scripture, "Zeal for your house will consume me."

The Jews then challenged him, "What sign can you show us to justify your doing this?" Jesus answered, "Destroy this temple, and in three days I will raise it up." The Jews responded, "This temple has taken forty-six years to build, and you are going to raise it up in three days!" But the temple he was talking about was the temple of his body. After he had risen from the dead, his disciples remembered that he had said this, and they believed the Scripture and the words that Jesus had spoken.

While Jesus was in Jerusalem for the feast of Passover, many people saw the signs he was performing and came to believe in his name. However, Jesus would not entrust himself to them because he fully understood them all. He did not need evidence from others about man, for he clearly understood men.

All of the four gospels describe the reaction of Jesus, in the Temple, when he drives out those selling animals, and the money changers. This tells us just how important this event was, and the disappointment of Jesus as he witnessed those making money, and therefore profit, for themselves, in the house of his Father. Hence, the moral of the story is easy for us to understand, in so far as, you cannot buy God's favour through purchasing, and offering sacrifices.

Yet, we must not forget how important the Temple was to the Jews because it symbolised the very presence of God with his people. This magnificent building, once the tallest in the world, meant that God dwelt with his people, and would always be with them, and never abandon them. John, however, in his gospel adds a conversation between Jesus, and the Jews, which the other gospels do not. It is here that Jesus, in fact, makes a remarkable claim; that if the Temple is destroyed, he will raise it up in three days. Little wonder, that when the Jews heard this, and looking at the Temple, which had taken decades to build, they were overcome with shock and dismay. John, however, tells us, *'Jesus was speaking of the temple of his body.'*

At this point, it is important to know, that when John wrote his gospel, the Temple in Jerusalem had been destroyed by the might, and power of the Roman Empire up to thirty years before. As a result, many of the Jews were left feeling lost and abandoned, as the unthinkable had happened, God no longer dwelt in the midst of his people. What were they to do now? Where could they go? How would they survive, as the people of the covenant?

John now steps into this void, with his gospel, and offers a way out, through the revelation of a remarkable truth. They can, in fact, now forget the old Temple because a new one has arrived in Jesus Christ. The old religious leaders had destroyed Jesus, as he said they would, but the Father raised him to new life, and in so doing, heralded a new relationship with God.

As a result, everything has now changed, for all those who recognise Jesus as the new temple. The emphasis, however, is not on cultic practices within a building but on a living relationship with God through Jesus. Hence, this new relationship is marked by the characteristics of *living in spirit and truth.* This means joining yourself to Jesus, and living in and through his *spirit* but the only way this can be done is by walking in his footsteps as one of his disciples. To do this, one must also grasp the truth, or good news, of his gospel.

John also reveals another remarkable truth, that the doors of this new temple are closed to no one. Hence, everyone is welcome, and no one is turned away. Here the emphasis is on inclusion, which means slaves as well as free people, Gentiles as well as

Jews, even the rejected, despised, unwanted and unloved sinners, are all welcome. In essence, John is telling the people, that something new is here, something never heard before, that God is the God of all people, and not the privilege of the few. If there is a condition, then it is reduced to the fact, that all that is required is a recognition of a need for God's love, which is given freely and unconditionally to all. This was something which had never been heard before and reveals the very heart of God. Little wonder, therefore, that Christianity spread so quickly amongst people who, up to this point in time, had been told that God had rejected and abandoned them. Perhaps then, the message is abundantly clear for those of us calling ourselves Christian today. That if we are to be authentic witnesses to Christ, we must recapture this fundamental truth of the gospel and make it live.

Something to think about and discuss:

1. *Why do you think the cleansing of the Temple is included in all four Gospels?*
2. *What does the cleansing of the Temple teach us about how the church is called to be an authentic witness to Christ in the world today?*
3. *In your experience is the church a place of welcome to all people? How might things, in your opinion, be improved?*
4. *In what way is Christianity good news for you?*
5. *As a Christian what do you think is meant by being an authentic witness to Christ?*

Four:

Love like God (agape – αγάπη)

John 3:14-21

Fourth Sunday of Lent

Jesus said to Nicodemus:

And just as Moses lifted up the serpent in the desert,
so must the Son of Man be lifted up,
in order that everyone who believes in him
may have eternal life.

"For God so loved the world
that he gave his only Son,
so that everyone who believes in him
may not perish
but may attain eternal life.

"For God did not send his Son into the world
to condemn the world
but in order that the world might be saved through him.
Whoever believes in him is not condemned,
but whoever does not believe in him
already stands condemned,
because he has not believed in the name
of the only-begotten Son of God.

"And the judgment is this:
the light has come into the world,
but people preferred darkness to light
because their deeds were evil.
Everyone who does evil hates the light
and avoids coming near the light
so that his misdeeds may not be exposed.
However, whoever lives by the truth
comes to the light
so that it may be clearly seen
that his deeds have been done
in God."

In today's Gospel reading we have a radical, and revolutionary statement about God's relationship with the world, *'For God so loved the world, that he gave his one and only Son, not to condemn the world, but to save the world through him.'* Such love is the source of all our hope because it is unconditional, and guarantees that we are not, in fact, alone. Rather, we are constantly surrounded by the love of God.

Yet, we have a problem because in English there is only one word for love. The New Testament and therefore the Gospels, on the other hand, were originally written in Greek where there are, at least, four words for love.

1. Philia – strong friendship-based love, such as that found in marriage.
2. Eros – romantic love.
3. Storge – family relationship love.
4. Agape (αγάπη) God or Christ like love, which is unconditional and self-emptying.

The highest form of love, therefore, is agape (αγάπη) because it reveals the nature of God's love. We see this love most perfectly revealed in Jesus, who because of his closeness to the Father, spends his whole life self-emptying, the unconditional love of God for the world. In the same way, this is the role of the church in the world today. As the body of Christ, and commissioned by him, the mission of the church is to communicate to humanity, God's unconditional, self-emptying, agape love, for all people. There is no more important role for the Church than this.

Returning to the Gospel itself, we are told that Jesus is given to the world by the Father as a gift. Hence, there is no condemnation here, but the world will, however, be saved through Christ. The emphasis, as a result, and the very essence of the Gospel to be preached by the Church, must be on agape love. In other words, the Church is not called to preach the Gospel of condemnation but only that of agape love. Whenever this is not adhered to, the danger is that the Church falls into the trap of preaching its own gospel of power, control, and manipulation, rather than that of Jesus Christ.

Finally, we can now come to our own role in what it means to be a Christian in the world today. First and foremost, our role is to respond positively to the invitation given to us by Christ, to follow him. This means, of course, to love, just like him. Hence, our commission is to love others with self-emptying, unconditional, agape love. In practice, this requires us to live good, authentic, Christian lives, bringing acts of mercy, compassion, forgiveness, and love wherever we go, but especially to those who suffer. It means to seek out all those who live on the margins, to include the excluded, and to put the needs of others before our own. Yet, we can only do any of this through the sure, and certain knowledge that we are, in fact, loved by God first.

Something to think about and discuss:

1. *Has your understanding of love changed because of reading this reflection? Can you give reasons as to why this might be the case?*
2. *How difficult is it to love like God in the world today?*
3. *Do you think the church continues to be an authentic witness to agape love?*
4. *In what way does the church have to change, if it is to reach out to those who have left or to those who have never heard the Gospel? What ideas do you have as to how this might be done?*
5. *Spend time reflecting on how you are loved, unconditionally, by God through his Son.*

Five:

Only Crucified Love Will Draw All People to God

John 12: 20-30

Fifth Sunday of Lent

Among those who had come up to worship at the feast were some Greeks. They approached Philip, who was from Bethsaida in Galilee, and said to him, "Sir, we would like to see Jesus. Philip went to tell Andrew of this, and Philip and Andrew informed Jesus. Jesus answered them,

"The hour has come
for the Son of Man to be glorified.
Amen, amen, I say to you,
unless a grain of wheat
falls into the earth and dies,
it remains just a grain of wheat.
However, if it dies,
it bears much fruit.

"Anyone who loves his life loses it,
but the one who hates his life in this world
will preserve it for eternal life.
If anyone wishes to serve me,
he must follow me.
Where I am,
there also will my servant be.
If anyone serves me,
my Father will honour that person.

"Now my soul is troubled.
Yet what should I say:
'Father, save me from this hour'?
No, it was for this
that I have come to this hour.
Father, glorify your name."

Then a voice came from heaven,

"I have glorified it,
and I will glorify it again."

The crowd that was present heard this, and some of them said that it was thunder, while others asserted, "An angel has spoken to him." Jesus answered,

"This voice did not come for my sake
but for yours.
Now is the judgment on this world.
Now the prince of this world
will be driven out.
And when I am lifted up from the earth,
I will draw all to myself."

He said this to indicate the kind of death he was to die.

In today's Gospel a group of people who, we are told, are Greeks, and therefore not Jews, approach the disciples of Jesus. Their request is a simple one, *'We want to see Jesus.'* When Jesus is informed of this, he responds by sharing, with his disciples, the meaning of his mission. Everything he tells them will culminate, with all people being drawn into the mystery of his love. However, for this to happen, he must die first, only then will God's love be fully, and finally revealed, for the entire world to see. Hence, he tells them, *'When I am lifted up from the earth, I will draw all people to myself.'* This, of course, is a direct reference to his crucifixion. In this way, the crucified God will reveal the depth of his love for all people, and they, in turn, will be drawn into the depths of that love.

When we turn to our own lives of faith, on this fifth Sunday of Lent, Jesus invites us to be drawn to him, and to lose ourselves in the love he has for each and every single one of us. Yet, at the same time, we must never forget that this is how God *feels* about all people. Or rather, this is how God *loves* all people. Such a belief or way of relating to God must, therefore, impact on our humanity, and the way in which we live our lives, especially the way in which we relate to our fellow human beings.

Theologians tells us, that God the Father, and God the Son, loved each other perfectly, and that Jesus, at the moment of his death, surrendered himself totally to the Father. At the same time, this also revealed God's love for humanity, and that Jesus's greatest desire was that we should share in his relationship with his Father too, by putting all our faith and trust in him. Perhaps, this all begins with recognizing our need for God's love as revealed in his Son, Jesus Christ, through his death on the cross. Out of this, emerges a deeper desire, not only to love him, but to serve him. This can only be done, however, by living authentic Christian lives, which clearly reveal something of the nature of God's love for all people. Only such witness can align itself with the crucified God, who died for all people. Listen again to the words of Jesus from today's Gospel reading, *'Whoever wants to serve me, let him follow me, and where I am there my servant will also be.'*

Loving God, and loving all people go hand in hand. To be a disciple of Jesus, in the world today, means to walk in his footsteps, to share in his mission, to participate in his life, and even to share in his fate. In simple language, the Christian is called to incarnate, make present, Jesus in the world today. So that, *'where I am, there will my servant be.'* This is demanding stuff for both individual Christians, and the church, because it requires us to love as he did. Imagine that, loving all people, no matter who they are, like God does. This is exactly what it means to walk in the footsteps of Jesus, even when it takes us to the cross. Yet, we must never forget that wherever we go, and whatever we do, we share in his life, and are loved unconditionally by his self-emptying, all-inclusive, love. Now imagine a church like that, drawing all people to the crucified God; what a sight that would be for our broken world today.

Something to think about and discuss:

1. *Why do you think Jesus had to die to reveal the depths of God's love?*
2. *What does the crucified Jesus tell us about God?*
3. *Do you believe that through your faith in Jesus you share in the life of God, and are, therefore, loved, unconditionally by him? How would you explain this to someone else?*
4. *How would you define a disciple of Jesus in the world today?*
5. *In your opinion, is the church you know drawing people to the crucified God? Try to give reasons for your answer.*

Six:

Living a Life of Crucified Love

Mark 14:1-15:47

Passion (Palm) Sunday

It was now two days before the Passover and the feast of Unleavened Bread, and the chief priests and the scribes were seeking to arrest Jesus by deceit and put him to death. They said, "It must not occur during the feast, or the people may begin to riot."

When Jesus was in Bethany reclining at table in the house of Simon the leper, a woman came in with an alabaster jar of very costly ointment, made of pure nard. She broke open the jar and poured the ointment over his head. Some of those present said to one another indignantly, "Why was this ointment wasted in such a manner? It could have been sold for more than three hundred denarii, with the money given to the poor." And they began to rebuke her sharply.

However, Jesus said, "Let her alone! Why are you bothering her? She has performed a good action toward me. The poor you will always have with you, and you can show kindness to them whenever you wish, but you will not always have me. She has done what she could. She has anointed my body to prepare for my burial. Amen, I say to you, wherever in the whole world this gospel is proclaimed, what she has done will be told in remembrance of her."

Then Judas Iscariot, who was one of the Twelve, went to the chief priests and offered to hand him over to them. They were delighted when they heard his proposal, and they promised to give him money. Then he began to look for an opportunity to betray him.

On the first day of the feast of Unleavened Bread, when it was customary to sacrifice the Passover lamb, the disciples said to Jesus, "Where do you want us to go and make the preparations for you to eat the Passover?"

He sent forth two of his disciples, instructing them: "Go into the city, and a man carrying a jug of water will meet you. Follow him! Wherever he enters, say to the master of the house, 'The Teacher asks: "Where is the room where I can eat the Passover with my disciples?"' Then he will show you a large upper room furnished and ready. Make the preparations for us there."

People often ask me, especially children, *why did Jesus have to die?* The answer to this, however, is not easy but as we reach Passion Sunday, and enter Holy week, it gives us the opportunity to reflect on this all-important question.

The first point to make, is that Jesus spent most of his time with the despised, unwanted, and rejected. Such groups were mainly made up of what the scriptures call sinners; that is to say, prostitutes, tax-collectors, the poor, the crippled, the diseased and the unloved. To the outrage of the religious leaders of the day Jesus assured such people of two things, that they were loved unconditionally by God, and that they would be first in the Kingdom of Heaven. In other words, Jesus revealed a God who included everyone and excluded no one. Indeed, it is possible to conclude that he deliberately identified himself with the most wretched, and despised people, which even included slaves. All of this, set the religious leaders of the day against him because they believed in a God who was exclusive to them, who rejected, and even punished sinners. By aligning himself with slaves, Jesus even risked the wrath of the Roman Empire.

However, none of this mattered to Jesus because he was merely being faithful to his Father's will, even when that risked his own life. Hence, throughout his ministry Jesus would tackle, head on, injustice and suffering. He cured the sick, raised the dead and brought healing and consolation to all those who suffered. Equally, he forgave sin and confronted a religious aristocracy which sought power, prestige, wealth, and status for itself, by manipulating and controlling the people of God. Little wonder, therefore, that when they saw the special position given to them by Rome threatened by this itinerant preacher from Galilee, they plotted to kill him.

The Gospels tell us, repeatedly, that Jesus knew his death was inevitable, if he continued with the mission given to him by his Father. Yet the Kingdom of Heaven had to be preached, and the God of mercy, compassion, forgiveness, and love revealed. Never before had humanity heard the unconditional, self-emptying, all-inclusive love of God proclaimed in this unique way. Its message was both radical and outrageous. To declare, openly, that both the poor and sinners were unconditionally loved by God and given first place in the Kingdom of heaven was, inevitably, a call for radical change. For those only interested in maintaining the status quo, however, it meant that Jesus had to go.

Ultimately, Jesus would die the death of a common criminal, even that of a slave, on the cross. Yet, his death sealed a bond between God, and suffering humanity, for all time. In essence, it was an act of pure love both for his Father, and for all those broken by life. At the same time, his death brings salvation to all those seeing themselves as lost. In him and through him, the excluded will always be welcome, the sick will find comfort and consolation, and all victims of injustice and oppression will be raised up. In and through the cross of Jesus Christ, the forgiveness, and mercy of God, are both assured.

These are the reasons why we are drawn to the cross because in the crucified Jesus, we see not only our Lord offering his life, as an act of pure love, to the Father and to us, but we also see ourselves. Out of the cross, therefore, pours the unconditional love of God for all people, for all time. Remember what we said in our previous reflection, *'When I am lifted up from the earth, I shall draw all people to myself.'* Turning to the cross today then, as we prepare to enter Holy Week, perhaps we need to do so with a sense of joy in our hearts as we gaze upon this incredible symbol of God's love for us, and for all people. Yet equally, we should be emboldened by the fact that Jesus shares both his life, and his mission with us, to go out into the world, and to live the life of crucified love.

Something to think about and discuss:

1. *Spend some quiet time in front of a crucifix and try to explain what it means to you.*
2. *If an honest enquirer asked you why did Jesus have to die, what would you say?*
3. *In your own words describe the God revealed by Jesus Christ.*
4. *How can Christians, and the church, continue the mission of Jesus in the world today?*
5. *Why do you think we celebrate Passion Sunday at the beginning of Holy Week?*

Mark and Easter

'Do not be alarmed. You are looking for Jesus of Nazareth, who was crucified. He has been raised. He is not here.'
(Mark 16:6)

Seven:

Experiencing the Risen Lord

Mark 16:1-17

The Vigil

When the Sabbath was over, Mary Magdalene, Mary the mother of James, and Salome purchased aromatic spices so that they might go and anoint Jesus. And very early on the first day of the week, just after sunrise, they went to the tomb.

They had been asking each other, "Who will roll back the stone for us from the entrance to the tomb?" But when they looked up, they observed that the stone, which was extremely large, had already been rolled back. On entering the tomb, they saw a young man arrayed in a white robe sitting on the right-hand side, and they were stunned.

He said to them, "Do not be alarmed. You are looking for Jesus of Nazareth, who was crucified. He has been raised. He is not here. See the place where they laid him. But go forth and tell his disciples and Peter: 'He is going ahead of you to Galilee. There you will see him just as he told you.'"

A question I often get asked is, *'How can I experience the resurrection of Jesus?'* Easter, in fact, answers this question; now we need to find out how. You see, the answer is staring us right in the face, in the Gospel reading for today, but we need to take the time to really look.

Our reflection begins with three women who simply cannot let go of their love for Jesus. Hence, Mary Magdalene, Mary the mother of James, and Salome are making their way to the tomb to anoint the body of their beloved Lord. On arriving, and to their great surprise, they find that the stone has been rolled away and the tomb is empty, the body of Jesus nowhere to be seen. Instead, they see a young man, dressed in white, who reveals something to them beyond their wildest dreams. He begins, however, with a question, *'You are looking for Jesus of Nazareth, the one who was crucified?'* Before going on to reveal a remarkable truth. It is wrong to seek Jesus in the world of the dead. Hence, Jesus is not here, and their search to find his body quite fruitless. So, do not weep for that which you cannot see, instead realise the one you seek is risen, and will now live for all time. Yet, other questions remain for the women, *'Where is Jesus, and will they ever see him again?'* To this, the young man gently reminds them of something Jesus has already told them, *'He is going to Galilee, ahead of you; there you will see him.'* Perhaps, at this point, we could pause, and reflect for ourselves, on what the young man is inviting the women to do. Why are they told to return to Galilee to see the Risen Lord, and what has this got to do with us?

Casting our minds back, Jesus spent most of his earthly ministry in Galilee. It was there he called his disciples, preached, healed, and proclaimed the Kingdom of Heaven. A Kingdom of unconditional love, where even sinners could find a home. Eventually, such a life lived in complete conformity to the will of his Father would lead to the cross, crucifixion, and even death. There is no escaping this. Hence, if we are to truly experience the resurrection of Jesus and his risen life, then we must first of all take up our own cross and walk in his footsteps. Only by attempting to live a life of faith, and therefore conforming our lives to that of Jesus, will we ever, truly, be able to experience his resurrection. Such a road will never be easy but only by striving, and even struggling to live in such a way, especially in moments of darkness, pain, and isolation, will we ever realise that God is, in fact, closer to us than we could ever imagine, and loves us more than we could ever know. This is the point of our whole Lenten journey, and everything has been leading us to this moment.

Ultimately, on this great and glorious Easter day, God invites us to see, and believe, that Jesus lives in us. As we journey through life, therefore, we must forgive like him, heal like him and, of course, love like him. This was the whole point of telling the women to go back to Galilee, where it all started. Our faith tells us, however, that as we make this journey, through life, we are never alone because our risen, and glorified Lord, goes before us. If then, we are ever to experience the resurrection of Jesus, it all starts with accepting his invitation, to follow him.

Something to think about an discuss:

1. *What does Easter mean to you?*
2. *How can we experience the resurrection of Jesus in our own lives today?*
3. *What does it mean to accept the invitation, given to us by Jesus, to follow him?*
4. *How can we be authentic witnesses to Christ in the world today?*
5. *Where would you place hope as an essential ingredient to discipleship? Can you give reasons for your answer?*

Eight:

Depending and Living on the Presence of Jesus

John 20:19-31

Second Sunday of Easter

On the evening of that same day, the first day of the week, the doors of the house where the disciples had gathered were locked because of their fear of the Jews. Jesus then came and stood in their midst and said to them, "Peace be with you." After saying this, he showed them his hands and his side.

The disciples were filled with joy when they saw the Lord. "Peace be with you," Jesus said to them again.

"As the Father has sent me,
so I send you."

After saying this, he breathed on them and said,

"Receive the Holy Spirit.
If you forgive anyone's sins,
they are forgiven.
If you retain anyone's sins,
they are retained."

Now Thomas, called the Twin, who was one of the Twelve, was not with the rest when Jesus came. When the other disciples told him, "We have seen the Lord," he replied, "Unless I see the mark of the nails on his hands and put my finger into the place where the nails pierced and insert my hand into his side, I will not believe."

Eight days later, the disciples were again in the house, and on this occasion, Thomas was with them. Although the doors were locked, Jesus came and stood in their midst, and he said, "Peace be with you." Then he said to Thomas, "Put your finger here and see my hands. Reach out your hand and put it into my side. Do not doubt any longer but believe." Thomas exclaimed, "My Lord and my God!" Then Jesus said to him,

"You have come to believe
because you have seen me.

Blessed are those who have not seen
and yet have come to believe."

Now Jesus performed many other signs in the presence of his disciples that are not recorded in this work. But those written here have been recorded so that you may come to believe that Jesus is the Christ, the Son of God, and that through your belief you may have life in his name.

Today, in our Gospel reading, we find out what really transformed the lives of the disciples. It was nothing less than the presence of the risen Lord in their midst. At once all their fears disappear as they experience, only the peace, which Christ can give. As they are touched by the breath of Jesus their hearts are filled with great joy. Only now did they understand, therefore, that the mission given to Jesus by his Father was their mission too. Knowing, and believing, that Jesus would always be with them they walked out through the door, which had been previously closed, and with them the church was born.

I often take great comfort from the words of Saint Ambrose who once said something like, *the further from the fire we go the colder and darker it becomes.* In other words, whatever you do, stay close to Christ, which is where we find the disciples in this morning's Gospel reading. This, however, is what must become a reality in our lives too, if we are ever going to continue the mission given to the church by Jesus. We must recognise that the resurrected Christ is at the heart of his church, and this must have an impact on everything that we do. It sounds simple but we must learn to love again the risen Lord present in our midst, just as those disciples did all those centuries ago, because everything depends on this.

How do we know, however, when this is happening? Once again, the answer is simple, because the church community begins to reflect, something of the nature of its risen Lord, on whom its whole life depends. Yet, everything begins with faith in the risen Christ who is the source of all our hope and joy. You see such a church simply lives according to the values of the Gospel where everyone is valued and included, where the lost can find a home, and where power, manipulation, and control have no place. Such a church is sensitive and empathetic to people's needs, it listens, comforts, and consoles those broken by life. Yet, it draws all its strength from its risen Lord. Only the risen Christ can do this, and hence, staying close to him is imperative. It is for this reason, that the church has nothing to fear in or from the modern world. Remember that the first words of Jesus to his disciples after the resurrection was, *'Do not be afraid.'* In fact, these words occur no less than 365 times in the Bible, one for every day of the year. By always turning to Christ and seeing him at the very heart of the church there is, in truth, nothing to fear, especially when we recall his final words to the disciples in Matthew's Gospel, *'I am with you always till the end of time.'*

If we fail to do this, however, we will be consumed by the crisis which threatens to overwhelm us. Pope Francis, constantly tells us, that we are to be a people of *'joy.'* Our hearts must be set on fire by that flame of most perfect love, so that others, may be warmed, by our faith. Yet, our starting point must always be with recognising how much we need Jesus. By turning to him constantly, and feeding off his living presence, as the disciples did, our lives will, literally, overflow with his love. Only Jesus can give us the strength we need. Only Jesus can fill our hearts with joy, and only Jesus can give true meaning, and purpose, to our lives. On this second Sunday of Easter then, we need to rediscover an enthusiasm for the living presence of Jesus in our midst, and turn to him, allowing his peace to flood our hearts, to shape our lives, and inspire our every deed.

Something to think about and discuss:

1. *In today's Gospel reading why do you think the disciples of Jesus were still afraid?*
2. *What changed the disciples and why were they, 'overjoyed?'*
3. *As disciples of Jesus today in what ways are we afraid?*
4. *In the reflection, find the quote from Saint Ambrose and reflect on what it means for you.*
5. *How can the church rediscover, today, the truth, that Jesus is present in our midst? Why is this so important?*

Nine:

I Want to Believe

Luke 24:35-48

Third Sunday of Easter

Then the two described what had happened on their journey and how he had made himself known to them in the breaking of the bread.

While they were still conversing about this, Jesus himself stood in their midst and said to them, "Peace be with you." Startled and terrified, they thought that they were seeing a ghost.

He said to them, "Why are you troubled, and why are doubts arising in your hearts? Look at my hands and my feet. It is I myself. Touch me and see. For a ghost does not have flesh and bones as you can see that I have." And when he had said this, he showed them his hands and his feet.

In spite of their joy and amazement, they were still incredulous. So, he said to them, "Do you have anything here to eat?" They gave him a piece of fish, and he took it and ate it in their presence.

Then he said to them, "This is what I meant when I told you while I was still with you: Everything written about me in the Law of Moses, the Prophets, and the Psalms must be fulfilled." Thereupon, he opened their minds to understand the Scriptures.

And he said to them, "Thus it is written that the Christ would suffer and on the third day rise from the dead, and that in his name repentance and forgiveness of sins are to be proclaimed to all nations, beginning from Jerusalem. You are witnesses to all these things.

Believing in the resurrection of Jesus is not easy, and it is not something which usually happens overnight. For some people, it is a process which can take many years, and this in itself should give us some comfort. Our starting point needs to be with our desire to completely trust Jesus by making a clear space for him in our hearts because when we do this, wonderful things can happen. You see faith is a free gift, given to all of us by Christ, and it is what we do with it which counts. It may help, therefore, to see our faith as something fragile and, at times, vulnerable. Many of us have doubts and uncertainties, life is hard, and we may have been continuously knocked down. Hence, we very often find ourselves struggling to believe in that ultimate victory over darkness, resurrection. Today's Gospel reading comforts us by revealing the fact that even for the disciples who were physically present with Jesus, belief in his resurrection was a slow process, as he gradually opened their minds. So, what is good enough for the disciples has to be good enough for us, right? The fact is that Jesus was preparing his disciples to speak and preach in his name, but the only way they could do that was by drawing on their own interior experience of the resurrection. Let us now explore how Jesus did this, and then apply it to our own lives of faith today.

Going back to that room, all those centuries ago, presents us with an interesting scenario. The disciples came together, all expressing their own experiences of the resurrection. Two of them explained how they had encountered the risen Jesus, on the road, as they journeyed to Emmaus. Indeed, he had actually stayed, and shard a meal with them. Peter recounts what had happened to him, whilst others are still to have any kind of first-hand resurrection experience at all. Then all of a sudden, Jesus is standing there, amongst them saying, *'Peace be with you.'* Once again, the disciples are experiencing his presence. This then is the key to everything, including that of our own faith. For we too must realise that the gift of faith, planted deep within our hearts, by Christ himself, enables us to experience his risen presence here and now. Once this happens our lives become flooded with the sure and certain knowledge that, in the words of Saint Matthew, *'God-is-with-us.'* This, in turn, brings the kind of peace, and joy, that the world cannot give, and must be reflected in the way in which we live.

Yet, going back to Saint Luke, it is interesting to note that the presence of Jesus, even in the midst of his disciples does not transform them straight away. How honest and realistic is that. Rather, we discover that some of them are afraid, others that they are, in fact, seeing a ghost, and some even continued to have doubts. So, if this okay for the disciples who were in the presence of the resurrected Jesus, then it must be all right for us today too. Putting it simply, sometimes we struggle with believing, and God knows that. See how Jesus invites those present in that room to touch him, and even to eat with him, to allay their doubts and fears.

So, what we are learning from today's Gospel reading, as we move further and further away from the rush of the excitement of Easter day, is that there is no one right, and exclusive way, to experience the resurrection of Jesus. It may, as we have said, take many years but the desire to believe and trust in Christ, with all our hearts, will expand the seed of faith living within us to one day burst forth into the light, just as Jesus did on that first Easter morning.

Something to think about and discuss:

1. *Read this morning's Gospel reading slowly for yourself and highlight anything you find surprising.*
2. *Describe you own belief in the resurrection.*
3. *Why do you think some of the disciples found it so difficult to believe that Jesus had risen from the dead?*
4. *How would you explain, to an honest enquirer, why the resurrection is so important to the Christian faith?*
5. *Is there a difference between believing in the resurrection, and experiencing it?*

Ten:

'The Smell of the Sheep'

John 10: 11-18

Fourth Sunday of Easter

"I am the good shepherd.
The good shepherd
lays down his life for the sheep.
The hired hand,
who is not the shepherd
nor the owner of the sheep,
sees the wolf approaching,
and he leaves the sheep and runs away,
while the wolf catches and scatters them.
He runs away
because he is only a hired hand
and he has no concern for the sheep.
"I am the good shepherd.
I know my own,
and my own know me,
just as the Father knows me
and I know the Father.
And I lay down my life for the sheep.
"I have other sheep too
that do not belong to this fold.
I must lead them as well,
and they will hear my voice.
Thus, there will only be one flock,
one shepherd.
"This is why the Father loves me,
because I lay down my life
in order to take it up again.
No one takes it away from me.
I lay it down of my own free will.
And as I have the power to lay it down,
I have the power to take it up again.
This command I have received from my Father."

Referring to the Roman Catholic priesthood, Pope Francis made the comment that priests should be so close to the people they have been called to serve, that they should be like shepherds with their sheep. At the time, in which Jesus lived, shepherds spent the vast majority of their lives out on the hillside with their sheep. Indeed, such was their relationship, that each sheep would have its own name, and would recognise only the unique cry of its shepherd. By day he would lead them to pastures of fresh, green grass, and streams of clear water. Whilst at night, the shepherd would herd his flock into a sheepfold, a semi-circular enclosure, made out of stone, with no solid door. Instead, the shepherd, himself, would lie across the entrance with only his crook, as a defence, against the wild animals which would seek the sheep as their prey. In this way, the shepherd would, literally, be willing to lay down his life for his sheep. Now, perhaps, we can begin to make sense out of what Jesus said, *'I am the good shepherd, I know my sheep and my sheep know me and I lay down my life for my sheep.'*

Traditionally, Bishops have adopted the role of shepherds in the church with their crook as a tangible symbol of their office. However, it is possible, to apply the shepherd image, to any such leadership position. Yet, wherever this does happen, the shepherd must conform their pattern of leadership to that of Jesus, the good shepherd. Think back now to what we said a little earlier about the life of the shepherd at the time of Jesus:

- Constantly present with the sheep
- Always by their side with their best interests at heart
- Providing for them, feeding, and sustaining them
- Never leaving or abandoning them
- Protecting them
- Willing to lay down his life for them

Remember how we also said that the shepherd knows each of the sheep by name, such is his closeness to them? Yet equally, they also know him. Perhaps, we could describe such a relationship in terms of union, oneness, or even communion. I know this sounds idealistic, but it comes to us directly from Jesus himself. This image of mutual *'knowing'* could even be described in terms of intimacy such is the bond presented to us. What better way, therefore, could there possibly be to describe leadership roles in the church today than this? Here we see people and leaders working closely together, guided by the grace of the Holy Spirit, and the values of the Kingdom of Heaven, to build a church, which will truly be a light to the nations because it is based on mutual and reciprocal love.

However, is this really the image of the church today? How much time do we spend arguing with each other? How often do we talk about good Catholics, bad Catholics, and lapsed Catholics, liberal or conservative Catholics? Shamefully how much energy is wasted on deciding whether we support the Pope or not? The list could go on, but it all seems far removed from the image of Jesus, the good shepherd, knowing and loving each of his sheep.

You see Jesus made some things abundantly clear, that the shepherd *knows* his sheep because he loves them. Hence, the model for leadership in the church today, particularly those occupying high office, is based on intimacy and familiarity. When this happens a sense of togetherness is created because the sheep, that is to say, the people of God, literally know that their leaders, that is to say, the bishops, will do anything for them. Here there is no room, for a *them and us* approach because leaders, *'know the smell of their sheep.'* They share their hopes and dreams, their successes, and failures, they can speak their language, which is never patronising but grounded in experience, and welcome dialogue rather than imposition as a way of communicating with people. In this way, everyone is valued but above all else, everyone is loved because the sheep *know* that their shepherd will lay down his life for them.

We should never be afraid to return to the scriptures to discover, sometimes for the first time, what God is saying to us. Jesus does not compromise in what he expects the shepherd to do for his sheep. First and foremost, we are the people of God, and belong to him. Shepherds are called, not to live in ivory towers, but to be in the midst of God's people ministering to their needs, in Christ's name. He is their model, and will guide, strengthen, and sustain them through the grace of his Holy Spirit, as they serve the people of God. In this way, the pilgrim church can move ever forward offering a different way of being to the world but at its heart will always be Christ, the good shepherd.

Something to think about and discuss:

1. *What do you think Pope Francis meant by, 'The smell of the sheep?'*
2. *How effectively is leadership in the church today modelled on Christ the good shepherd?*
3. *Do you think there is a close link between the church hierarchy, Archbishops and Bishops, and the people they are called to serve?*
4. *Reflect on your own experience of church leadership. How has it been received, and what suggestions might you make for improvement?*
5. *What do you think makes for an effective church leader when it comes to Archbishops and Bishops?*

Eleven:

Cling to Jesus

John 15:1-8

Fifth Sunday of Easter

Jesus said to his disciples:

"I am the true vine,
and my Father is the vine grower.
He removes every branch
that does not bear fruit,
and every branch that does
he prunes to make it bear even more.
You have already been cleansed
by the word I have spoken to you.

"Abide in me,
as I abide in you.
Just as a branch cannot bear fruit by itself
unless it abides in the vine,
so you cannot bear fruit
unless you abide in me.

"I am the vine,
you are the branches.
Whoever abides in me, and I in him,
will bear much fruit.
Apart from me you can do nothing.
Whoever does not abide in me
will be thrown away like a withered branch.
Such branches are gathered up,
thrown into the fire, and burned.

"If you abide in me
and my words abide in you,
you may ask for whatever you wish,
and it will be done for you.
By this is my Father glorified,
that you bear much fruit
and become my disciples."

As we move further, and further away, from Easter day, our initial enthusiasm begins to wane. Hence, todays Gospel reading reminds us that, above all things, we must always cling to Christ. Spending time reflecting on what John has to say can refill our spiritual tanks, as it were, by taking us to the imagery of the vine and its branches. Only Jesus is the *'true vine,'* and we are the branches, constantly living off the life-giving sap which only he can provide. At the same time, think of the Father as the one who looks after the vineyard, making sure it brings forth an abundant harvest. In this way, everything is directed towards achieving the peace, and salvation, of the whole world.

At the same time, however, we are also presented with another reality, which, perhaps, many of us are tempted to skip over. Notice, that on the vine some of the branches have gone dry. This is because they are no longer receiving the life-giving sap given to them by Jesus. When this happens, the harvest is impoverished, and there is no fruit. Is this a warning given to us by Jesus? His words suggest it is, *'a branch cannot bear fruit if it does not abide in the vine.'* In other words, *'apart from me you can do nothing.'* Perhaps, we need to stop here, and really take on board what Jesus is actually saying to us. Putting it simply, whether it be individuals, our parish, the diocese, or the whole church, without Christ we can do, literally, nothing. If then there is ever a crisis, whatever form it may take, our initial reaction must always be to examine our relationship with God, in Christ, first.

Today we are being told, in no uncertain terms, that a living relationship with Jesus is vital, if we are to authentically bear witness to him. Jesus must be at the heart, the very core, of everything that we do. After all, is not the Gospel good news, and are we not compelled to live our lives in accordance with it? Forget this, and what are we? Water this down, and what are we offering people? Christ is our unique gift, he is our lifeblood, and without him our lives lack meaning. Imagine a church which forgets this? What has it become? Today then, we need to go back to the Gospel, and really listen, to what God is saying to us, and incorporate it into every fibre of our being, *'apart from me you can do nothing.'* Think about what Jesus is saying to us today. Every moment, every second of your life, I am pouring my life-giving Spirit into you. I am closer to you than you could ever imagine, and I love you more than you could ever know. Now go, and in my name, change the world.

In conclusion then, Jesus must live in our hearts because he simply offers his life to us. Or putting it another way, through Christ we, literally, share in the life of God. This, however, must be reflected in the way in which we live our lives, and this can only be done when we become increasingly aware of just how close Jesus is to us. Deep within the depths of our being lies the source of who we really are, and Jesus invites us to experience him there. If we forget this for too long, the danger is, we become like dry branches on the vine, and look what happened to them. Hence, it is vital, that we '*remain in him,'* and when we do that, all will be well.

Something to think about and discuss:

1. *Describe how you feel about your faith as we reach the Fifth Sunday of Easter. Has anything changed since Easter Sunday?*
2. *What does the image of the vine and the branches mean to you?*
3. *Reflect on your thoughts about what happens to the dry branches. What do you think Jesus is saying to us through this image?*
4. *Reflect on your own relationship with Jesus, how might it be deepened?*
5. *What can the church learn from today's Gospel reading?*

Twelve

I call you Friends – Love one Another

John 15:9-17

Sixth Sunday of Easter

"As the Father has loved me,
so have I loved you.
Remain in my love.
If you keep my commandments,
you will remain in my love,
just as I have kept my Father's commandments
and remain in his love.

"I have told you these things
so that my joy may be in you
and your joy may be complete.

"This is my commandment:
love one another
as I have loved you.
No one can have greater love
than to lay down his life for his friends.
You are my friends
if you do what I command you.

"I shall no longer call you servants,
because a servant does not know
what his master is doing.
I have called you friends
because I have revealed to you
everything that I have heard from my Father.

"You did not choose me.
Rather, I chose you.
And I appointed you
to go out and bear fruit,

fruit that will remain,
so that the Father may give you
whatever you ask him in my name.
The command I give you is this:
love one another."

Our Gospel reading for today, is part of what is called the farewell discourse, as Jesus prepares his disciples for when he will no longer be, physically, with them. Hence, here we find how Jesus wants them to live, if they are to be faithful, living witnesses to him, and his mission. It is, therefore, vital that we understand, that what Jesus says to his disciples, he also says to us.

Above and beyond everything else, Jesus exhorts us, first and foremost, to *'Remain in my love.'* Here Jesus invites us to know, and believe, that every moment, every second of our lives we are loved unconditionally by him. Imagine that; Jesus desires that we know, that just as the Father loves him, so he loves us. Such love cannot, and will not, ever come to an end, by knowing, believing, and living our lives with this truth in our hearts, life takes on a whole new dimension. As a result, on this Sixth Sunday in the season of Easter, all of us should spend some time simply resting in the arms of God's love.

We can now move on to explore what this means for our lives of faith. Once again, Jesus tells us, quite simply to, *'keep his commandments.'* At this point, perhaps, we need to take a breath so that we can really take on board what Jesus says next. This is because, in truth, Jesus only ever gives his disciples one commandment and it is this, *'love one another as I have loved you.'* Here we find, summed up, everything Jesus wants us to know about what it really means to accept his invitation to be one of his disciples. All we have to do, is love others, in the same way, he loves us. There is no commandment greater or more important than this. Indeed, Jesus makes the point even further, when he says, *'others will know that you are one of my disciples by the love you have for each other.'* Putting it simply, the mark, sign and symbol of Christian discipleship, the ultimate test of its true authenticity, is unconditional love.

Now let us give some time to thinking about what impact, living in this way, should have on our lives. Once again, I go back to the words of Pope Francis when he said, that Christianity should be lived with *'joy'* in our hearts. After all, how will it ever be attractive to others, if they cannot see what an effect that living our lives, knowing we are loved unconditionally by Jesus, has on us? Indeed, Jesus himself makes this exact same point when he says, *'I say this to you so that my joy may be in you and that your joy may be full.'* It is here that we find a pattern for living which gives meaning to everything we do. Knowing that we are loved first by Christ must be reflected by the love we have for others, only this can bring true joy to our hearts. When we see life in this way everything changes because every moment has the potential to realise, make present, the love of God.

The key, of course, is that God loved us first. He came in search of us, to find us, simply because he loves us, there is no other reason. In this way Jesus invites us into an intimate relationship with him, and in so doing calls us, *'friends.'* Now we are able to see the face of Christ, literally, everywhere, whilst at the same time knowing, and believing, that he lives in and through us. This enables us to put all our fears to one side, and live lives of simple joy. Think about what happens when all of this is absent. What impression will others get of our Lord if we fail to love like him, and practice our faith without joy? Today then, we need to realise two things, firstly that Jesus only gives us one commandment, to love others in the same way he loves us, and there is nothing more important than this. And secondly, that he calls us his *friends.* If this does not fill our hearts with joy, then, perhaps, nothing will.

Something to think about and discuss:

1. *Spend some time, today, realising how much you are loved, unconditionally, by God. Why is this so important?*
2. *Jesus only gives us one commandment, to love others in the same way he loves us. What do you think this really means?*
3. *Why do you think Jesus calls his disciples, and in turn us, friends?*
4. *Reflect on the role of joy in your own faith. What conclusions do you come to?*
5. *Think about the church, how can it reflect, more effectively, the teaching of Jesus, found in the Gospel for today?*

Thirteen:

Above All Things - Trust in God

Mark 16:15-20

Ascension of the Lord

Then he said to them, "Go forth into the whole world and proclaim the gospel to all creation. Whoever believes and is baptized will be saved; whoever does not believe will be condemned. These are the signs that will mark those who believe: In my name they will cast out demons. They will be granted the gift of speaking in new languages. If they pick up serpents in their hands or drink any deadly poison, they will remain unharmed. The sick on whom they lay their hands will recover."

Then, after he had spoken to them, the Lord Jesus was taken up into heaven, and there he took his place at the right hand of God. And they went forth to proclaim the gospel everywhere, while the Lord worked with them and confirmed the word by means of the signs that accompanied their preaching

As we reach Ascension Day, and move ever more closely, towards the end of the Easter season, it is vital that we continue place all out trust in God. This, in fact, is something Jesus, himself, urges us to do. At times, it is tempting to become despondent as we see not only the church fighting against, and within itself but droves of our loved ones leaving. When this happens, it is vital to remember that God is not confined to his church, and also operates in the world, and therefore outside of it. For this reason, we can be consoled by the fact that God's grace continues to work in the hearts, minds, and lives of our loved ones who no long practice their faith. Remember the parable of the lost sheep? God never abandons anyone – fact! The sheep may be lost but God never stops loving them. Thus, even though the church might appear to be moving painfully slow, at times, wracked by dispute and division, God's grace is always at work both inside, and outside of it. All this serves to highlight the importance of putting all our faith, hope, and trust, in the living God.

Now let us explore how this is linked to our Gospel reading for today. Mark, in his version of the Ascension, is making a very important point, which at first sight is easy to miss. We find it in the words of Jesus to his disciples just before he leaves them, *'Go into all the world and preach the good news to all creation.'* Here Jesus is telling us, directly, that his gospel is for all people, or in other words, it is meant to be inclusive, and not exclusive. In these words, we find an imperative or a demand for the disciples, and in turn the church, to take the gospel to the ends of the Earth. However, have we lost this momentum today through becoming too inward looking, as our loved ones increasingly drift away?

Jesus tells us not to lose heart because the Father is still at work both inside, and outside of his church. This brings us back to the need to place all our hope, and all our trust in him. Remember, the words of the Our Father, includes all people and excludes no one. It is God who comes in search of us, it is always he who makes the first move, because he is our Good Shepherd, closer to us than we could ever imagine, and loving us more than we could ever know. Yet, this brings with it, a responsibility, to be ambassadors for Christ, in the world. You see other people might not read the Bible, but they will read us. Even though our faith in Jesus might not change we may have to think of new ways of communicating that faith to others. What we do must never do, however, is become a barrier to those seeking Jesus. Our parishes, our churches, and our hearts must, always be open to those on the outside looking in. Will they find in us a place of warmth, and welcome? Will they find in us lives fuelled by the gospel of life? Will they recognise in us the face of Christ himself? Ultimately, the gospel has a power in itself, which comes only from God. Yet, he entrusts it to us, not to keep it to ourselves but to offer it to others in his name. If we are to do this, then first and foremost, we must learn, again, if necessary, to place all our hope, and all our trust in God.

Something to think about or discuss:

1. *What does Ascension Day mean to you and your life of faith?*
2. *Reflect on your own experience of loved ones or people who you know leaving the church. Can you think of reasons why they did this?*
3. *Jesus tells his disciples to, 'Go out into the world and preach the good news.' What does this mean for you?*
4. *Without compromising the truth of the faith how can the church preach the good news today? What ideas do you have?*
5. *Reflect on what it means to place all our trust in God. Is this something, which we all need to rediscover? If so, can you suggest, how we might go about this?*

Fourteen:

Holy Spirit – Dwell in our Hearts

John 20: 19-23

Pentecost

On the evening of that same day, the first day of the week, the doors of the house where the disciples had gathered were locked because of their fear of the Jews. Jesus then came and stood in their midst and said to them, "Peace be with you." After saying this, he showed them his hands and his side.

The disciples were filled with joy when they saw the Lord. "Peace be with you," Jesus said to them again.

"As the Father has sent me,
so I send you."

After saying this, he breathed on them and said,

"Receive the Holy Spirit.
If you forgive anyone's sins,
they are forgiven.
If you retain anyone's sins,
they are retained."

If there is one theme, which has run through these Easter reflections, it is our need to stay close to Christ. Above, and beyond all things, Jesus, needs to be at the very heart of our lives, for in the words of Saint Paul, *'Without him we can do nothing.'* As we reach the end of the Easter season, Jesus pours out the gift of the Holy Spirit on his disciples, and in turn us too. It is something that we can easily forget but note what Jesus says to his disciples first, *'As the Father has sent me, I am sending you.'* Imagine that, we are given the same mission by Christ that his Father gave to him. Our response to this can only be one of humility, and excitement, and yet everything depends on receiving the gift of the Holy Spirit. Today then, let us turn with a renewed sense of enthusiasm to the Holy Spirit, and allow it to stir up within us, afresh, a desire to share directly in the mission of Jesus himself for the salvation of the whole world.

So, what then should our priorities be? Think of it, perhaps, like this:

To be totally dependent on the Holy Spirit as the constant presence of God within our lives.

To make sure that Jesus is always at centre of everything we do whether that be as individuals, parishes, or the church.

To recognise that there is no higher law than that of compassion or love.

To feed constantly on God's word and sacrament.

To place, just as Jesus did, all our hope, and all our trust, in God our heavenly Father.

To believe that God loves all people unconditionally, and that we should reflect this in our lives of faith.

To form communities which include all people and exclude no one.

To be instruments of God's peace, by seeking out the lost, the lonely, and all those living on the margins.

To be deeply concerned about the suffering of others, and do whatever we can, to relieve their pain.

To be on the side of people in need, to be a voice for the voiceless, and to provide a safe place of refuge for the vulnerable.

To stand up for justice, truth, decency, honesty, and integrity.

To recognise that we are not, in fact, perfect but very often weak, fragile, and sinful, just like everybody else.

To walk alongside those who are struggling, and to be there when they stumble and fall.

To make every effort to see, and engage, with the world through the eyes of Christ, and to act as he would.

I could, of course, go on because there is no end to such a list. Yet, everything comes down to recognising how Christ, invites us, to share in his mission, to be part of creating a better world. A more humane or Christ like world. This was the task given to him by his Father and passed directly on to us through the grace of the Holy Spirit. On this Pentecost Sunday, let us pray that the Holy Spirit is poured, once again, into our hearts, reviving within us, a sense of meaning, and purpose, to engage with the world in the name of Christ our Lord and Saviour. Let us do so with joy, and the certain knowledge that he is closer to us than we could ever imagine, and loves each and every single one of us, more than we could ever know. At first, we might be afraid but so were the disciples in today's Gospel reading. Knowing this, Jesus simply said to them, and in turn to us, *'Peace be with you.'* Then he gave them the gift of the Holy Spirit. Little did they know then, what an adventure they would face, and here we are. Now it is our turn, and who alone, but the Father, knows where we will be led but that in itself should be enough because it is in him that Jesus invites us to place all our hope, and all our trust, just as he did.

Something to think about and discuss:

1. *What does the Holy Spirit mean to you and what role does it play in your life of faith?*
2. *Reflect on what it means to be part of Christ's mission for the salvation of the world.*
3. *Thinking about the list in today's reflection which of them, if any, do you find yourself most attracted to. You can, of course, choose more than one.*
4. *What role does fear play in preventing us from living our lives in accordance with the teachings of Jesus?*
5. *Spend some time reflecting on the words of Jesus to his disciples and in turn to us, 'Peace be with you.'*

Year C:
Luke

Luke and Lent

'This is my Son, the Chosen One, listen to him.'
(Luke 9:35)

One:

'Until Christ is Formed in You' (Galatians 4:19)

Luke 4:1-13

First Sunday of Lent

Jesus, full of the Holy Spirit, returned from the Jordan and was led by the Spirit in the wilderness, where for forty days he was tempted by the devil. He ate nothing at all during those days, and when they were over, he was famished. The devil said to him, "If you are the Son of God, command this stone to become a loaf of bread." Jesus answered him, "It is written, 'One does not live by bread alone.'"

Then the devil led him up and showed him in an instant all the kingdoms of the world. And the devil said to him, "To you I will give their glory and all this authority; for it has been given over to me, and I give it to anyone I please. If you, then, will worship me, it will all be yours." Jesus answered him, "It is written,

'Worship the Lord your God and serve only him.'"

Then the devil took him to Jerusalem, and placed him on the pinnacle of the temple, saying to him, "If you are the Son of God, throw yourself down from here, for it is written,

'He will command his angels concerning you, to protect you,' and 'On their hands they will bear you up, so that you will not dash your foot against a stone.'"

Jesus answered him, "It is said, 'Do not put the Lord your God to the test.'" When the devil had finished every test, he departed from him until an opportune time.

I am going to begin this reflection with some remarkable words of Jesus found in the Gospel of John, *'As the Father has sent me, so I am sending you.'* (John 20:21) Imagine that Jesus is telling us, that we share directly in his mission. Or putting it another way, Jesus entrusts the mission given to him by his Father, to us. This, therefore, is something we must be faithful to. Yet there is a problem that many people today are often tempted to dismiss, and it is that of evil or as Luke tells us, in today's Gospel, the devil.

There can be little doubt that the primary aim of the devil is to distract or tempt Jesus away from the mission given to him by his Father. If we are to be faithful to the mission given to us by Jesus, then it is essential that we recognise that we face the same temptations as he did. Only by being faithful to Jesus, therefore, will we be able to see such temptations for what they really are, and resist them.

The first temptation invites Jesus to turn stones into bread in order to satisfy his own hunger. Let us now reflect on what this actually means for us today. We, like Jesus, must not give into the temptation to place our own needs, and interests first. Rather, and again like Jesus, we must respond to such a temptation in two ways. Firstly, we need to turn to the living word of God found in the scriptures and allow ourselves to be nourished by them. Whilst secondly, and again following the example of Our Lord, rather than satisfying our own hunger, we should be listening, and responding to, the cries of the starving in our world.

In the second temptation, found in Luke, Jesus refuses to accept the power, and glory offered to him by the world. How often in the world today does such power lead to abuse, corruption, and injustice? The Kingdom of God has nothing to do with any of these. Instead, its priorities are mercy, compassion, forgiveness, and love. Hence, those who commit themselves to the mission of Jesus can never be concerned with power, control, or manipulation. After all, did Jesus not spend the majority of his earthly mission with the poor, weak and despised of the world? This means that the church, and all those who belong to it are called, and invited by Jesus, to be something different. A community which makes up his living body on earth, committed to his mission, as brothers and sisters called to reveal his unconditional love for all people. To achieve this, we cannot give into that which the world appears to respect, power, status, success, and wealth. In resisting such temptation, we are aligning ourselves with Jesus the humble, and obedient servant of his

Father. Here we find the pattern for our own lives too, and in so doing, conform our way of life to his.

When we turn to the final temptation, once again, we discover Jesus rejecting the devil's attempt to seduce him into accepting the mantle of a triumphant Messiah. After all, was this not what the people expected? A Son of David, a soldier and a warrior, a man who could be adored and followed by the masses. A triumphant warrior king who would defeat all the enemies of God. This was someone, who at last, the entire world could recognise, and look up to. Surely this was Jesus's destiny. How often are we tempted to capitulate when it comes to conforming to what others expect of us? How easy would it be just to give into how the world measures and recognises success? Yet Jesus, in rejecting all such things makes something abundantly clear. He will, under no circumstances, use his Father, to achieve his own, vain glory. Or putting it another way, self-glorification has nothing to do with the Kingdom of Heaven or the mission of Jesus Christ. In fact, for Jesus the reverse is true. Time and time again, Jesus makes it very clear to his disciples that he is amongst them as one who serves. Indeed, he washes their feet, the actions of a common bond slave, to make this point, and invites them, and in turn us, to do the same for each other. Hence, if the world seeks to recognise and reward fame, reputation, and prestige, then we must reject it. But what we are left with is far more powerful. By aligning ourselves with Jesus, and rejecting all the temptations of the devil, we become part of his mission which is the transformation of the whole world. Lives of humble service, revealing the unconditional love of God for all people, is what Jesus invites us to do. Such lives, lived in conformity to the Gospel draw their energy from Jesus who lovingly says to each, and every single one of us, *'As the Father has sent me, so I am sending you.'*

Something to think about and discuss:

1. *Spend some time reflecting on the meaning of, 'As the Father has sent me, so I am sending you.'*
2. *Why do you think many people, today, do not take the existence of the devil seriously?*
3. *Thinking about the first temptation of Jesus, reflect on the role, and importance of the scriptures in your own life of faith.*
4. *When it comes to the second temptation of Jesus, how difficult is it to reject all that the world has to offer in terms of power, status, and wealth?*
5. *The life of the Christian is an invitation to be different. How difficult, therefore, is it to live the life of a humble servant of God, in the world today?*

Two:

The Uniqueness of Jesus

Luke 9:28-36

Second Sunday of Lent

Now about eight days after these sayings Jesus took with him Peter and John and James and went up on the mountain to pray. And while he was praying, the appearance of his face changed, and his clothes became dazzling white. Suddenly they saw two men, Moses, and Elijah, talking to him. They appeared in glory and were speaking of his departure, which he was about to accomplish at Jerusalem. Now Peter and his companions were weighed down with sleep; but since they had stayed awake, they saw his glory and the two men who stood with him. Just as they were leaving him, Peter said to Jesus, "Master, it is good for us to be here; let us make three dwellings, one for you, one for Moses, and one for Elijah"—not knowing what he said. While he was saying this, a cloud came and overshadowed them; and they were terrified as they entered the cloud. Then from the cloud came a voice that said, "This is my Son, my Chosen; listen to him!" When the voice had spoken, Jesus was found alone. And they kept silent, and in those days told no one any of the things they had seen.

The transfiguration is one of the events found in the Gospels which the evangelists attached huge importance to. What we are presented with today, through Luke's eyes, is an insight into the unique identity of Jesus. Let us now reflect on what this passage is, in fact, telling us. The first thing to note, is what happens to the face of Jesus and Jesus alone, when Luke describes the transfiguration. His face is transformed, and his clothes became as white as lightening. With him stand Moses representing the Law, and Elijah, the Prophets. Although they appear in glorious splendour, only the face of Jesus is transfigured as he stands in their midst.

At this point Peter speaks out, as he often does, and in so doing makes a grievous error. For he declares, *'Master it is good for us to be here. Let us put up three shelters – one for you, one for Moses and one for Elijah.'* Now can you see the mistake that Peter makes? In effect he treats all three of them as equals when plainly they are not. Could it be, therefore, that at this point in his discipleship Peter is still yet to grasp the uniqueness of who Jesus really is? As if to put the record straight it is God the Father who now speaks out, and at the same time corrects Peter's error by pronouncing, *'This is my Son, whom I have chosen.'* Or in other words, do not confuse Jesus with anyone else, look only his face is transfigured. Moses and Elijah only reflect the light of which Jesus is the source. You must, therefore, *'Listen to him,'* and him alone.

There can be little doubt that the account of the telling of the transfiguration had a huge impact on the life of the early church. Hence, it is preserved and retold in Matthew, Mark, and Luke. Here we begin to understand the uniqueness of the Gospels for Christianity. As such, they are unlike any other piece of literature because they declare openly that Jesus is the Christ, the Son of the living God. It is for this reason that we must treasure them treating them with the dignity, and respect they deserve. After all, they not only contain the eternal word of God but are the very words of life itself.

As a result, we must rediscover something that our brothers and sisters found in the Gospels all those centuries ago – the uniqueness of Jesus. In reading the Gospels we can see the impact Jesus firstly had on his disciples, to the point that they, literally, left everything and followed him. Equally, we can relive those moments when others were touched by his healing presence. In following Jesus through the Gospels, we discover God's unconditional love for the poor, the weak, the outcast and the sinner. We find our brother, our friend, and our Lord. Ultimately, the face of God, himself, is painted for us by the authors of the Gospels as we are led on a journey through his mission to save the world.

Recently Pope Francis made the point that ultimately the Christian faith is not about doctrines, law, or theology but it is about a person, and that person is Jesus Christ, the unique Son of God. Who simply invites us to follow him, and if truth be told, to fall in love with him. On this second Sunday of Lent, we need to spend some time reflecting on the uniqueness of Jesus, and follow the instructions given to us by the Father to simply, *'Listen to him.'* After all, in doing so, we are hearing the words of God himself, and only he can guide us through the maze of life. In a world which often appears lost, bombarding us with information through a multitude of media where the truth is often compromised. We can, however, be sure of one thing, that when we listen to Jesus we are, in fact, directly hearing the word of God, speaking to the very depths of our soul.

Something to think about or discuss:

1. *What does the account of the transfiguration mean to you?*
2. *How would you describe your relationship with Jesus?*
3. *What role do the Gospels play in your life of faith?*
4. *Spend some time in prayer reflecting on the uniqueness of Jesus.*
5. *In what ways do you find yourself challenged by today's Gospel reading?*

Three:

Where Was God and Where Were You?

Luke 13:1-9

Third Sunday of Lent

At that very time there were some present who told him about the Galileans whose blood Pilate had mingled with their sacrifices. He asked them, "Do you think that because these Galileans suffered in this way, they were worse sinners than all other Galileans? No, I tell you; but unless you repent, you will all perish as they did. Or those eighteen who were killed when the tower of Siloam fell on them—do you think that they were worse offenders than all the others living in Jerusalem? No, I tell you; but unless you repent, you will all perish just as they did."

Then he told this parable: "A man had a fig tree planted in his vineyard; and he came looking for fruit on it and found none. So, he said to the gardener, 'See here! For three years I have come looking for fruit on this fig tree, and still, I find none. Cut it down! Why should it be wasting the soil?' He replied, 'Sir, let it alone for one more year, until I dig around it and put manure on it. If it bears fruit next year, well and good; but if not, you can cut it down.'"

This is one of those parables, which if I am perfectly honest, at first sight, I struggle with in terms of understanding its meaning. For this reason, I have placed it within the wider context of the whole passage from Luke.

So, a man plants a fig tree, and leaves it to be looked after by someone else. After three years of care the tree still fails to produce fruit so the owner decides to cut it down. At this point, his servant intercedes on behalf of the tree arguing that, if after one more year of his careful care, the tree still fails to bear fruit it can then be cut down. Or in other words the servant is asking the owner to give the tree one more chance to produce fruit. What can this possibly mean?

Firstly, let us look at what happens in the passage immediately prior to the parable. A group of unknown people approach Jesus telling him that under the orders of Pilate some Galileans have been killed, and their blood mixed with that of animals being sacrificed and offered to God. Why did these people tell Jesus this? What motivated them to come to him? What were they expecting his reaction to be? What were they hoping for? Did they, perhaps, think that such people must have done something to offend God to warrant such a horrific death? If this were not the case then how come if the victims were, in fact, innocent, would God allow such an awful thing to take place in the temple?

The response of Jesus to this appears, at first sight, to be quite strange. He tells them about another set of events, which again took place in Jerusalem, and involved the death of eighteen people who were crushed when a tower, close to the pool of Siloam, collapsed. What, however, does all this mean, and how are the two incidents connected? Perhaps, Jesus is making the point that in both cases those who died were no less or no more guilty than anyone else living in Jerusalem. As a result, the section finishes with these words, *'Unless you repent, you too will perish.'* In other words, Jesus is suggesting that they should take the opportunity of recognising who it is standing before them and change their ways; just like the fig tree was given one more year to bear fruit.

Here, Jesus clearly rejects any suggestion that disasters are to be interpreted as punishments sent from God, which was, in fact, one of the prevailing views of the day. In this way, Jesus also makes something abundantly clear, that any teaching that even suggests God punishes sin by sending sickness, poverty, or death, is wrong. So, what does all this mean then? How are we to make sense out of the disasters which not only come our way in life but, which very often, strike also at the heart of those people least able to cope? How can we now make sense out of it all?

When disaster strikes, no matter what it is, we might be tempted to react by asking, *'where was God? How can a loving God allow such things to happen? Why doesn't this all-powerful God do something?'* Indeed, in my visits to schools, these are the very questions young people immediately fire at me when we are discussing natural disasters.

Yet Jesus is teaching us that these are the wrong questions, instead we should be asking ourselves, *'where was I?'* Or putting it another way, we should let God ask us, *'where were you?'* In this way, such incidences become opportunities to change our lives, to become more compassionate, to become more human, and to become more like Christ.

When we are confronted with any kind of disaster but particularly those which impact on the poorest people on earth, we should be challenged to ask a range of uncomfortable questions of ourselves. *Why are some people so desperately poor, and therefore least able to cope when natural disasters strike? Why are there such inequalities in the world resulting in untold human suffering? Why, when there are enough resources, including food, to go around we simply refuse to share? Why do we allow or turn a blind eye to so much human suffering and misery?* The answers to all these questions, which we may not like, comes from God, *'where were you?'* This then is the driving force behind the parable, God gives us all, one more chance, to do something. The challenge is to discover God in that place where we never thought of looking for him, in all those victims, in all those who suffer, and in all those who cry out to us in pain.

This is how Saint Mother Teresa put it:

'I used to pray that God
would feed the hungry, or will do this or that,
but now I pray that he will guide me
to do whatever I'm supposed to do,
what I can do.
I used to pray for answers,
but now I'm praying for strength.
I used to believe that prayer changes things,
but now I know that prayer changes us
and we change things.'

If the parable of the fig tree teaches us anything, it is that God always gives us another chance to act but there is not an option to do nothing.

Something to think about and discuss:

1. *Does God punish people?*
2. *What is our response, as people of faith, when disasters happen?*
3. *Reflect on what you believe is the most important teaching of Jesus. Be prepared to provide reasons for your answer.*
4. *When disasters happen where, according to Jesus, should we look to find God?*
5. *What is meant by, 'The God of second chances?' How important is this, in our understanding of the Father, revealed by Jesus?*

Four:

Some Uncomfortable Home Truths

Luke 15:1-3, 11-32

Fourth Sunday of Lent

Now all the tax collectors and sinners were coming near to listen to him. And the Pharisees and the scribes were grumbling and saying, "This fellow welcomes sinners and eats with them."

So, he told them this parable:

Then Jesus said, "There was a man who had two sons. The younger of them said to his father, 'Father, give me the share of the property that will belong to me.' So, he divided his property between them. A few days later the younger son gathered all he had and travelled to a distant country, and there he squandered his property in dissolute living. When he had spent everything, a severe famine took place throughout that country, and he began to be in need. So, he went and hired himself out to one of the citizens of that country, who sent him to his fields to feed the pigs. He would gladly have filled himself with the pods that the pigs were eating; and no one gave him anything. But when he came to himself, he said, 'How many of my father's hired hands have bread enough and to spare, but here I am dying of hunger! I will get up and go to my father, and I will say to him, "Father, I have sinned against heaven and before you; I am no longer worthy to be called your son; treat me like one of your hired hands."' So, he set off and went to his father. But while he was still far off, his father saw him and was filled with compassion; he ran and put his arms around him and kissed him. Then the son said to him, 'Father, I have sinned against heaven and before you; I am no longer worthy to be called your son.'_But the father said to his slaves, 'Quickly, bring out a robe—the best one—and put it on him; put a ring on his finger and sandals on his feet. And get the fatted calf and kill it and let us eat and celebrate; for this son of mine was dead and is alive again; he was lost and is found!' And they began to celebrate.

'Now his elder son was in the field; and when he came and approached the house, he heard music and dancing. He called one of the slaves and asked what was going on. He replied, 'Your brother has come, and your father has killed the fatted calf, because he has got him back safe and sound.' Then he

became angry and refused to go in. His father came out and began to plead with him. But he answered his father, 'Listen! For all these years I have been working like a slave for you, and I have never disobeyed your command; yet you have never given me even a young goat so that I might celebrate with my friends. But when this son of yours came back, who has devoured your property with prostitutes, you killed the fatted calf for him!' Then the father said to him, 'Son, you are always with me, and all that is mine is yours. But we had to celebrate and rejoice, because this brother of yours was dead and has come to life; he was lost and has been found.'"

The church deems this parable so crucial to our understanding of God that it is read to the faithful twice in Cycle C of the liturgical year. Yet it can make for an uncomfortable read, and it is easy to neglect the importance of the father, and his love for both sons, which of course reflects his love for us.

In this reflection I am, however, going to concentrate on the older of the two sons. He is the one who stays by his father's side, the faithful one who cannot for the life of him understand the attitude of his younger brother. When he hears of his wayward brother's return his initial reaction is bafflement as he learns of the party being given by his father to celebrate the reunion. However, this soon turns to anger and frustration when we are told, *'He became angry and refused to go in to join the feasting.'* He was the one who had remained loyal, staying by his father's side for all these years, and this is how he is repaid.

At this point, let us turn to the father summoned by his older son who is refusing to join in with all the festivities. He greets his son only with love and assures him that everything he owns is his too. The father reveals his nature of loving humility willing to treat both of his sons in the same way regardless of the mistakes they might make in life. There is no anger or frustration in the father, his words and manner speak only of compassion. Perhaps, it is this which breaks the older son because now he must let his father know how he really feels. In anger and frustration everything now pours out of him, how all these years he had stayed by his father's side working hard on the land. He had done everything he thought his father had wanted him to do unlike, of course, his younger brother who had done exactly the opposite. So why the welcome back? Why the party? Why all the celebration and festivities? Why reward wrongdoing? It is not fair, it is not just, it is not right, and it does not make sense! What the older son is really saying, is demanding from his father what he believes he deserves, what is his by right, what he has earned. Yet amid all this the one thing he has failed to learn is how to love, like his father.

Most of the commentaries, and reflections on this parable invite us to identify with the younger son, the sinner who repents, and comes home but here I want us to concentrate our attention on the older brother. He knows how to work the land, to do what is expected of him, and to stay by his father's side but he fails to understand how to love. To this end, he cannot comprehend how his father can still love his younger brother who abandoned them and squandered half of the family's estate. To him this just does not make any sense. As a result, he cannot welcome his brother back nor can he forgive him, in fact the implication is that he does not want to have anything to do with his brother at all. If you return to the parable for a moment, have a look at the ending because it might surprise you. There is no resolution. We do not know what happens next, and Jesus obviously wants us to reflect deeply on that.

This now brings us back to the church in the modern world, and to the initiative of Pope Francis who has invited the people of God to listen, and discern together, as to what the Holy Spirit is calling the church to be and do, given the times in which we live. This is, perhaps, where we need to be courageous, and listen to '*some uncomfortable home truths.*' What if we, as the church, identify with the older son in the parable, and are being looked at by the modern world, what do they see? Well first, we believe we live close to God, and are doing what he wants us to do. We have stayed loyal to the church and have not left, unlike most people. But what are we doing? The parable reveals that to stay close to God means to be like him filled with his mercy, compassion, forgiveness, and love for all people. This then leads to asking some rather uncomfortable questions such as, how welcoming are we as Christian communities? How willing are we to reach out to those who have either left the church or who have never seen themselves as part of it? Are we comfortable in encouraging people to question when they have doubts and walk alongside them, journeying together in search of the God of infinite love? How aware are we of the barriers we often put up which discourage people from approaching us because they are unable to see in our lives the God who turns no one away? How obsessed are we with maintaining what we have rather than with what we are called to be?

The parable teaches us something profound about God, which Jesus invites us to reflect in our lives of faith both as the church, and as individuals. That God loves all people equally, without exception, and that he has no favourites. That God's love cannot be earned because it is given as a gift. That God's love is overwhelmingly generous, and that once given it will never be taken back. That God only knows how to be merciful, compassionate, forgiving, and loving. If we could somehow live lives like that then the world would be changed. If the church could bear authentic witness to such a Gospel, then people would come.

Yet we spend so much of our time almost doing the opposite. We give people labels and identify them as either for us or against us. Think about it, we talk about practicing and lapsed Catholics, conservative and liberal Catholics, believers, and unbelievers, hence people are either in or out, part of us or not part us, one of us or not one of us, even good Catholics, and bad Catholics. Will we ever learn?

I have called this reflection *'The Father's Love,'* because ultimately this is the core meaning of the parable. God does not label us or differentiate between us because he simply loves *us*. And when I say he loves *us,* I mean all of *us*, without exception. Some people find this incredibly difficult to grasp, comprehend or even believe, just like the older son. Yet when all is said and done, we do not own God, he does not belong to us, he is not our property, but he is *Our Father,* and he loves *us* all, more than we could ever know.

Something to think about and discuss:

1. *Some people find it difficult to believe God loves all people unconditionally. How would you respond to this?*
2. *How would you sum up the main meaning of this parable?*
3. *What is meant by the 'mystery of the Father's love?'*
4. *As we reach the Fourth Sunday of Lent what challenges for both the church, and our own lives of faith, are to be found in this parable?*
5. *Spend some time reflecting on, and praying about, the meaning of, 'Our Father.'*

Five:

Jesus, Women, and the Church

John 8:2-11

Fifth Sunday of Lent

Early in the morning he came again to the temple. All the people came to him, and he sat down and began to teach them. The scribes and the Pharisees brought a woman who had been caught in adultery; and making her stand before all of them, they said to him, "Teacher, this woman was caught in the very act of committing adultery. Now in the law Moses commanded us to stone such women. Now what do you say?" They said this to test him, so that they might have some charge to bring against him. Jesus bent down and wrote with his finger on the ground. When they kept on questioning him, he straightened up and said to them, "Let anyone among you who is without sin be the first to throw a stone at her." And once again he bent down and wrote on the ground. When they heard it, they went away, one by one, beginning with the elders; and Jesus was left alone with the woman standing before him. Jesus straightened up and said to her, "Woman, where are they? Has no one condemned you?" She said, "No one, sir." And Jesus said, "Neither do I condemn you. Go your way, and from now on do not sin again."

Today's Gospel reading was felt to be so controversial, in the early church, that it is absent from many of the ancient manuscripts. Why might you ask is this the case? The simple answer is that it is because of the stance which Jesus takes on women. So, let us start this reflection by being honest with ourselves. Here we are two thousand years later, and women are still the most oppressed, and persecuted group of people on the planet. When war strikes, in any part of the world, it is women who are assaulted and raped the most. In our own country, woman are afraid to walk the streets at night alone for fear of predatory men. Indeed, in 2022, 1.7 million women in the UK were victims of domestic abuse. There is a noticeable lack of women present in the decision-making process of the church. Often women occupy the lowest paid jobs with very little social status. It is women who are expected to give up careers to look after children. Whilst across the world it is young women who are often denied access to education, and involvement in any kind of political process, which might lead to a change of the status quo. Hence, it is women who are often denied a voice, whose human rights are violated, and who are systematically oppressed, persecuted, and abused by men. If this is an honest assessment of how things are today, what was the situation like at the time of Jesus?

Putting it simply, far worse. You see in the ancient world, within the context of Judaism, and we have to remember that Jesus was a Jew. Women were considered to be incapable of telling the truth, think Eve in the garden, and as a result, were not allowed to give evidence in a court of Law. With this in mind, we can now turn our attention to today's Gospel reading. A woman has been caught in the act of committing adultery. A group of Pharisees, exclusively men, with responsibility for teaching the Law of God, bring her before Jesus. Everyone present knows that the Law of Moses demands that this woman, if found guilty, should be stoned to death. Yet, where is the man involved in this adulterous act? He, in fact, is never mentioned. Hence, what we are left with is a male dominated society, all too willing to identify the woman, exclusively, as the guilty party. The only thing left to do now is to get Jesus to agree with their verdict. Hence, appealing to the highest authority of all, they put this question to him, *'In the Law Moses commanded us to stone such women. Now what do you say?'*

What happens next, explains why this scene was excluded from so many of the ancient manuscripts, as male domination simply did not disappear with the coming of Jesus. Standing between the woman, and the men who condemned her, Jesus makes a stance, which comes directly from God, and speaks an eternal truth. It is the men who, in fact, are guilty but of hypocrisy based on male dominated arrogance. Hence, the death sentence, which they have condemned this woman to, does not come from God. It is Jesus, on the other hand, who will confront them with the truth. Applying the highest laws of all, compassion, mercy, and love.

Jesus reveals the truth, and justice of God in the woman's plight: *'If anyone of you is without sin, let him be the first to throw a stone at her.'*

The men are now confronted with their own shame and are forced to accept a hidden fact. It is they who are responsible for most of the adulteries which take place in their own society. It is this, that they must now accept responsibility for, which is why one by one they drop their stones and walk away. Now alone together, Jesus turns his attention to the woman, and speaking with tenderness and compassion simply says, *'Neither do I condemn you.'* Yet, it is important that something else happens here. Jesus makes it clear that the woman now has the opportunity to start her life anew. All she has to do is accept responsibility for her own life, and the way in which she lives it. Hence, Jesus concludes by saying, *'Go now and leave your life of sin.'*

What we are seeing here, through the way in which Jesus treats the woman, is the truth and justice of God in action. Exercising the law of mercy, and compassion, Jesus makes the point that it is not of God to respond to evil with evil. And yet here we are in the world today still seeing, right before our very eyes, the oppression of women. For example, an estimated 736 million or 1 in every 3 women experience some kind of abuse at the hands of men. Whilst, worldwide more than 650 million women alive today were married as children. Perhaps, given such frightening statistics it is not unreasonable to look to the church to provide a different model of behaviour. The first thing we need to do, is to be honest about the way in which the church has not always recognised, accepted, and used the full list of gifts and talents women possess. Then we need to go back to that image of the woman caught in the act of adultery by men, with Jesus standing between her and them. This is what Jesus calls his church, his body on earth, to be. Anything less than this is a betrayal of his Gospel.

Something to think about and discuss:

1. *Reflect on why today's Gospel reading was not present in some of the ancient manuscripts.*
2. *Now think about why, eventually, it was included.*
3. *What, if anything, have your learned from the reflection on today's Gospel reading?*
4. *Spend some time in prayer, with the Gospel for today, and see what happens.*
5. *How far do you agree or disagree with the conclusions made about women, in the life of the church, made in this reflection?*

Six:

The Crucified God

Luke 22:14-23, 56

Passion (Palm) Sunday

When the hour came, he took his place at the table, and the apostles with him. He said to them, "I have eagerly desired to eat this Passover with you before I suffer; for I tell you, I will not eat it until it is fulfilled in the kingdom of God." Then he took a cup, and after giving thanks he said, "Take this and divide it among yourselves; for I tell you that from now on I will not drink of the fruit of the vine until the kingdom of God comes." Then he took a loaf of bread, and when he had given thanks, he broke it and gave it to them, saying, "This is my body, which is given for you. Do this in remembrance of me." And he did the same with the cup after supper, saying, "This cup that is poured out for you is the new covenant in my blood. But see, the one who betrays me is with me, and his hand is on the table. For the Son of Man is going as it has been determined, but woe to that one by whom he is betrayed!" Then they began to ask one another which one of them it could be who would do this.

A number of years ago I wrote a book called, *'Only in the Crucified God – Questions and Answers on Faith, Hope, and Love.'* The premise was a simple one. To gather together some of the questions I had been asked, over the years, from both adults and children, those with faith and those without, and by simply using the Bible answer them. The only condition I attached to each of the questions, however, was that they must be answered only through faith in the crucified God.

Many Christians today often forget the scandal, and outrage involved in believing in the crucified God. Indeed, such belief, requires us to think in a completely different way, if we are to get anywhere near understanding what belief in such a God actually means. Indeed, to be both frank, and honest, many people both then, and indeed now, find it impossible to believe in a supreme being who would subject himself to the humiliating death of a common criminal.

So, this presents us with a number of challenging questions when attempting to answer any honest enquirer.

1. How is it possible for the Supreme Being, which is to say God, to be crucified by his own creation?
2. Why would God put himself through the humiliation of pain, suffering, and death?
3. What does all of this mean, and how can we make sense out of something which appears to be nonsense?
4. How can faith, based on a belief that the Son of God became human, and died the humiliating death of a common criminal, possibly survive?
5. What is God doing by dying on a cross?

If we are to understand any of this then we need to spend time, today, reflecting on our belief in a crucified God. The first thing we need to see is how such a belief turns upside down the expectations of the world. A crucified God is not a supreme, all powerful being, someone who is remote, and distant from our suffering. No! Rather he assures us that he suffers with us. That in all those moments of pain, grief, loss, anguish, heart ache, humiliation, darkness, and even death, he was there with us, sharing in every moment, and every second of what we went through. This is what we believe about the crucified God. Jesus actually comes to reveal or open up to us this new way of understanding his, and our Father. And why would God do this, the honest enquirer may well ask. Simply because he loves us in such a way that it is beyond our comprehension to understand.

In his death on the cross, Jesus removes all barriers between us and him, whilst at the same time, assuring us of his constant presence in our lives. Everything we go through, literally, in life, he experiences too. Indeed, Christ is telling us that our misery and pain, our sorrow, and tears, even the depths of our despair affect him. Wherever in the world suffering takes place God is there, not remote, or separate but intimately part of it. Hence, whenever we encounter suffering, of any kind, it is by its very nature an encounter with the crucified God. The challenge, therefore, is not to be believe in a remote, transcendent super being but to believe in the God who does not abandon us to pain, suffering, and even death but in the words of Saint Matthew, is God-with-us.

It is not surprising, therefore, that belief in the crucified God still challenges the world today because by its standards, and logic, it does not make sense. It is far easier to look away from the cross or to domesticate it than to embrace it as the truth. Yet today on this Passion Sunday, this is exactly what we are invited to do. Ultimately, an encounter with the crucified God is meant to change us by filling our hearts with his mercy, compassion, forgiveness, and love. Only when this happens can we be really sure that we have, in fact, had an encounter with the crucified God.

Something to think about and discuss:

1. *What do you think is meant by the term, 'The crucified God'?*
2. *Why do you think Catholics attach so much importance to the crucifix?*
3. *Reflect on the reasons why the crucifixion of Jesus is described in this reflection as an outrage, and a scandal.*
4. *Why do you think Jesus needed to go through the pain and agony of the cross?*
5. *How does the crucifixion of Jesus help Christians live a life of faith in the world today?*

Luke and Easter

'Why are you looking for the living among the dead?'
(Luke 24:6)

Seven:

'Why do you look for the living among the dead?'

Luke 24:1-12

Easter

But on the first day of the week, at early dawn, they came to the tomb, taking the spices that they had prepared. They found the stone rolled away from the tomb, but when they went in, they did not find the body. While they were perplexed about this, suddenly two men in dazzling clothes stood beside them. The women were terrified and bowed their faces to the ground, but the men said to them, "Why do you look for the living among the dead? He is not here but has risen. Remember how he told you, while he was still in Galilee, that the Son of Man must be handed over to sinners, and be crucified, and on the third day rise again." Then they remembered his words, and returning from the tomb, they told all this to the eleven and to all the rest. Now it was Mary Magdalene, Joanna, Mary the mother of James, and the other women with them who told this to the apostles. But these words seemed to them an idle tale, and they did not believe them. But Peter got up and ran to the tomb; stooping and looking in, he saw the linen cloths by themselves; then he went home, amazed at what had happened.

For me one of the most comforting, and faith affirming statements in the whole of the Bible, is found in today's Gospel reading. When the women enter the tomb on that first Easter morning, expecting to find the body of Jesus, which they had come to anoint, they encounter two angels. *'Why do you look for the living among the dead?'* they ask. *'He is not here; he is risen!'*

Yet, despite this, the disciples did not naturally, and immediately believe, in the depths of their hearts, that Jesus had, in fact, risen from the dead. Rather they were confused, experiencing doubts, and uncertainties about what it all meant. Perhaps, the simple truth is that nobody, not even then, believed that anyone could rise form the dead. Hence, Mary Magdalene looked for the crucified, and therefore dead body of Jesus, in the tomb in which he had been laid to rest. On discovering that the tomb is empty Mary does not believe that Jesus has risen from the dead. Rather, she is left feeling confused, and at a loss, as to where the body of Jesus is. So, at this point neither the group of women nor Mary Magdalene believe in a resurrected Jesus. Belief in the resurrection comes to them later, once they have had a direct experience of the risen Jesus, and time to reflect on what it all means.

What does faith in the resurrection of Jesus mean for us today then? Perhaps, the starting point has to be with our own honesty. As someone who has taught, and wrote about these things for many years, I would have to say, that it is extremely rare for anyone to embrace faith in the resurrection simply because they have been told about it or read about it in a book. I would say, however, that it is something we must experience for ourselves by undertaking our own spiritual journey. Where though do we look? Where do we search? How do we find such faith? The answer, in fact, is given to us in today's Gospel reading. We need to open our hearts and seek Christ with every fibre of our being. In every moment, in every experience, and in every person, we must search for Christ. But the key to everything is to look for him in the world of the living not of the dead because he is, in fact, alive.

To find, and experience the risen Jesus, we must look for him then at the heart of communities which gain their life from him. Here you will discover people living new lives infused with the resurrected life of Christ. Such communities will be identified by the loving service they have for each other whilst, at the same time, reaching out to those less fortunate than themselves. The risen, and glorified Lord will be at the heart of such communities living out his invitation to be people of mercy, compassion, forgiveness, and love. He will pour, constantly, his risen life into wherever two or three people gather together in his name, and they will reflect this by the way in which they live. This is how others will experience the resurrection of Jesus, here and now, by the love his followers have for each other, and for all people. Remember the words of the angel, *'Why look for the living among the dead?'* Jesus lives and seeks to touch our lives with his living presence. Indeed, only in him can the fullness of life be found.

The living Lord stands at the heart of our communities of faith whether that be our homes, our school, our parish, or any other place where people gather in his name. Such communities look to Jesus as their true source of life. In turn, this must be reflected not just in our relationship with him but with each other, as we seek to make present, in the here and now, his kingdom of peace, justice, and reconciliation for all people.

Something to think about an discuss:

1. *Describe your own belief in the resurrection of Jesus and what it means for your life of faith?*
2. *Why do you think the disciples of Jesus found it hard to believe he had risen from the dead?*
3. *Reflect on the words of the angel to the women in the tomb, 'Why do you look for the living among the dead?'*
4. *What does it mean to be a community of the resurrection today?*
5. *Does more time need to be spent, with people, helping them deepen their faith in the resurrected and glorified Lord?*

Eight:

'Stop doubting and believe.'

John 20:19-31

Second Sunday of Easter

When it was evening on that day, the first day of the week, and the doors of the house where the disciples had met were locked for fear of the Jews, Jesus came and stood among them and said, "Peace be with you." After he said this, he showed them his hands and his side. Then the disciples rejoiced when they saw the Lord. Jesus said to them again, "Peace be with you. As the Father has sent me, so I send you." When he had said this, he breathed on them and said to them, "Receive the Holy Spirit. If you forgive the sins of any, they are forgiven them; if you retain the sins of any, they are retained."

But Thomas (who was called the Twin), one of the twelve, was not with them when Jesus came. So, the other disciples told him, "We have seen the Lord." But he said to them, "Unless I see the mark of the nails in his hands and put my finger in the mark of the nails and my hand in his side, I will not believe."

A week later his disciples were again in the house, and Thomas was with them. Although the doors were shut, Jesus came and stood among them and said, "Peace be with you." Then he said to Thomas, "Put your finger here and see my hands. Reach out your hand and put it in my side. Do not doubt but believe." Thomas answered him, "My Lord and my God!" Jesus said to him, "Have you believed because you have seen me? Blessed are those who have not seen and yet have come to believe."

Now Jesus did many other signs in the presence of his disciples, which are not written in this book. But these are written so that you may come to believe that Jesus is the Messiah, the Son of God, and that through believing you may have life in his name.

I want to say something today to those people who might be struggling in their faith for all sorts of different reasons. However, let me start with something, which for some people might prove to be a little surprising. In today's Gospel John refuses to believe his fellow disciples when they tell him Jesus has risen from the dead. Instead, John wants proof! For the best part of a week John continues to wrestle with what he has been told others have experienced and seen about the risen Jesus. John, however, remains firm, and refuses to believe. Think about how many people you know are like John? Could there be something of John in all of us? Would that be wrong?

When Jesus does appear to John, he simply speaks words of love, *'Stop doubting and believe.'* It is at this point many people make a common mistake. John does not, according to today's Gospel reading, touch Jesus. He simply sees him and says, *'My Lord and my God.'* Yet, Jesus does invite him to, *'Put your finger here; see my hands. Reach out your hand and put it into my side.'* It would seem, therefore, that the invitation given to him by Jesus is, in fact, enough to lead John to faith. Ultimately, in this reading, we are seeing the movement of John's heart from doubt to belief as a result of an experience with his risen Lord.

For a moment or two now I would like to stay with John, and his week of scepticism. Recently a survey of Catholics, in the USA, revealed that fewer than 50% believed in the real presence of Jesus in the Eucharist. In the same way, many Christians doubt belief in life after death. It is also true that the number of church-going Christians, in the western world at least, has dramatically declined, in recent years. Yet, it is also true that people have become more insecure, and vulnerable, when it comes to hope for the future. As a result, it could be said that although, and quite rightly, people have become more critical and sceptical, it has not led to a more optimistic view of humanity. Yet, the invitation from Jesus made to each and every single one of us remains, *'Stop doubting and believe.'*

Perhaps, one of the things we have lost is that yearning for mystery. Instead, we have become obsessed only with that which we can see and touch. Putting it another way, humanity has become obsessed with itself, afraid to admit that there might be something beyond the tangible. When this happens, we become consumed by a darkness which refuses, even to be open to the possibility, that something might well exist beyond us. A mystery which, ultimately, is the true source of life itself. When this happens, we become lost, and life has no meaning, purpose, or value. At this point, death becomes final, and our yearning for mystery lost.

However, there is another way to look at life and death, and it is offered to us by Jesus. *'Stop doubting and believe,'* is what Jesus gently says to each and every single one of us. In fact, in these words, the same invitation given to Thomas is given to us. Here we discover an invitation to step into the mystery of God, which faith tells us is the ultimate reality. For those people reading this who might be struggling, all that is required is the desire, expressed in humility and sincerity, to simply seek God. Indeed, this in itself, is faith. You see very often we feel so weak and helpless, but God knows this, and if I am honest, it is the best place to start. Never forget that in the Gospel reading for today it is Jesus who went in search of Thomas. The same is true for us. It is God, through his son Jesus, who came to seek us out simply because he loved us first. Rest secure then, in the truth, that we are already in the arms of Jesus who gently and lovingly looks at us, and offers us the invitation to, *'Stop doubting and believe.'*

Something to think about and discuss:

1. *Being honest reflect on the ways in which you might be struggling with your faith?*
2. *Is it wrong to confess that, sometimes, believing in Jesus, and bearing witness to him is hard?*
3. *How is it possible, in the modern world, to rediscover our need for mystery when it comes to believing in God.*
4. *Again, and being honest, how much time do we spend in prayer, and reading the scriptures, when it comes to deepening our relationship with Jesus?*
5. *Spend some time contemplating the above reflection thinking about what you have found most helpful about it.*

Nine:

The Light of the World

John 21:1-19

Third Sunday of Easter

After these things Jesus showed himself again to the disciples by the Sea of Tiberias; and he showed himself in this way. Gathered there together were Simon Peter, Thomas called the Twin, Nathanael of Cana in Galilee, the sons of Zebedee, and two others of his disciples. Simon Peter said to them, "I am going fishing." They said to him, "We will go with you." They went out and got into the boat, but that night they caught nothing.

Just after daybreak, Jesus stood on the beach; but the disciples did not know that it was Jesus. Jesus said to them, "Children, you have no fish, have you?" They answered him, "No." He said to them, "Cast the net to the right side of the boat, and you will find some." So, they cast it, and now they were not able to haul it in because there were so many fish. That disciple whom Jesus loved said to Peter, "It is the Lord!" When Simon Peter heard that it was the Lord, he put on some clothes, for he was naked, and jumped into the sea. But the other disciples came in the boat, dragging the net full of fish, for they were not far from the land, only about a hundred yards off.

When they had gone ashore, they saw a charcoal fire there, with fish on it, and bread. Jesus said to them, "Bring some of the fish that you have just caught." So, Simon Peter went aboard and hauled the net ashore, full of large fish, a hundred fifty-three of them; and though there were so many, the net was not torn. Jesus said to them, "Come and have breakfast." Now none of the disciples dared to ask him, "Who are you?" because they knew it was the Lord. Jesus came and took the bread and gave it to them and did the same with the fish. This was now the third time that Jesus appeared to the disciples after he was raised from the dead.

When they had finished breakfast, Jesus said to Simon Peter, "Simon son of John, do you love me more than these?" He said to him, "Yes, Lord; you know that I love you." Jesus said to him, "Feed my lambs." A second time he said to him, "Simon son of John, do you love me?" He said to him, "Yes, Lord; you know that I love you." Jesus said to him, "Tend my sheep." He said to him the third time, "Simon son of John, do you love me?" Peter felt hurt because he said to him the third time, "Do you love me?" And he said to him, "Lord, you know everything; you know that I love you." Jesus said to him, "Feed my sheep. Very truly, I tell you, when you were younger, you used to fasten your own belt and to go wherever you wished. But when you grow old, you will stretch out your hands, and someone else will fasten a belt around you and take you where you do not wish to go." (He said this to indicate the kind of death by which he would glorify God.) After this he said to him, "Follow me."

Today's Gospel reading requires careful analysis if we are to understand what the Lord is saying to us. Perhaps, the first thing to point out, is how the reading constantly contrasts light with darkness. We begin with Peter who tells his fellow disciples, *'I'm going fishing.'* Or in other words, he is returning to his old way of life. After all, without the presence of Jesus what is he to do now? Without anything else to do his fellow disciples decide to go with him. Here Peter is taking the lead, and the disciples follow him but everything, or so it seems, takes place without the presence of Jesus. It is important to note, however, that all of this takes place at night, and therefore in darkness.

Moving on we discover that although they fished all night, *'they caught nothing.'* John, in his Gospel is, in fact, making a very important point, which is easy for us to miss. Which is, that in the darkness, and without the presence of Jesus, the light of the world, they can do nothing. You see the whole emphasis of this Gospel passage is really about evangelization or the spreading of the good news of Jesus Christ. Of course, they work hard but all their effort yields nothing. There is, as we shall see later, a very important message which John is trying to convey to us here. I wonder if you can, at this stage, work out what it is for yourself?

Everything changes when the light comes at dawn. It is at this point that Jesus appears on the shore and calls out to the disciples. However, they fail to recognise it is Jesus. Why could this be? So, he gives them a simple instruction, *'Throw your net on the right side of the boat.'* Immediately they discover that their net is so full they can hardly drag it back onto the boat. It is only at this point that they recognise that the stranger calling out to them from the shore is, in fact, Jesus. Did they recall those days long ago when he told them that by following him, they would become fishers of men? John is trying to tell us that successful evangelisation is not totally dependent on hard work and effort, as important as these may be, and which the disciples had been engaged in all night, but rather on the presence of Jesus.

Let us now see what happens when we apply this to our own lives of faith, and that of the church today. There can be little doubt that in many places the church is struggling with diminishing resources. The effect of this, very often, is that fewer, and fewer people are being asked to do more. It is at this point that we need to pause and evaluate what we are doing in the light of today's Gospel reading. What should our first priority be? To be successful and achieve predetermined targets or first and foremost to make sure we are maintaining the living presence of Jesus in our communities of faith. After all, the disciples worked all night, and caught nothing. It was only when Jesus appeared at dawn, and they followed his instructions, that they caught any fish.

This whole episode serves to remind us of something crucial when it comes to successful evangelization. Primarily we are called to bear witness to Christ because only he is the light of the world. Hence, we need to spend time developing our relationship with him as the source of our light and truth. Notice again how in today's Gospel reading everything changed, at dawn, when Jesus appeared on the shore, and the disciples followed his instructions rather than their own. Linked to this is the need to develop meaningful relationships in our own communities of faith, whereby everyone feels valued. When this happens, and with the risen Lord in our midst, we have a Gospel to offer, and evangelization can begin.

In other words, todays Gospel reading is, perhaps, asking us to reflect on what our priorities should be, as we seek to bring others to Christ. What is essential in our mission as the church of Jesus Christ? The starting point is not more activities, great effort, and hard work but simply coming together and listening to Jesus.

This is because if today's Gospel reading tells us anything, it is that without Jesus, who is the light of the world, we can do nothing.

Something to think about and discuss:

1. *Why do you think Peter, and the other disciples decided to go fishing in today's Gospel reading?*
2. *Why was it that the disciples failed to recognise Jesus as he called to them from the shore?*
3. *What do you think is the most important point being made by John in this Gospel passage?*
4. *Reflecting on your own life of faith, what have you learned from this reflection?*
5. *Thinking about communities of faith today, and the call to evangelization, what should our priorities be?*

Ten:

Listen to my Voice

John 10:27-30

Fourth Sunday of Easter

'My sheep hear my voice. I know them, and they follow me. I give them eternal life, and they will never perish. No one will snatch them out of my hand. What my Father has given me is greater than all else, and no one can snatch it out of the Father's hand. The Father and I are one.'

The world we live in today is very different to the one we were born into. We are constantly being bombarded with information at all times. There is 24-hour news, a whole range of social media and, of course, the internet. There is even something known, these days as fake news. All this means it is very difficult to know what to listen to, let alone believe. So, what are we to do? How is it possible to see through the images, slogans, claims, and counterclaims made every day? Where can we look for the truth? How can we dismiss the superficial? What sort of effect is this having on our faith?

The answer to all of this is, in fact, to be found in today's Gospel reading. When confronted with a group of religious leaders in the temple precincts, questioning his authority to teach and preach, Jesus responds to their lack of faith by using the image of a shepherd. At the time in which Jesus lived, shepherds knew their own sheep intimately to the point that each of them would recognise the distinct voice of their own shepherd. Hence, Jesus was able to say to the religious leaders who questioned his lack of authority, *'You do not believe because you are not my sheep.'* In response, many of them picked up stones to throw at him; such was their anger.

Yet, Jesus is not finished, and goes on to explain what it means to be one of his followers, *'My sheep hear my voice… and they follow me.'* The key for us, therefore, is that we must do the same. That is, listen to the voice of Jesus, and follow in his footsteps. Going back to the image of the shepherd, at the time of Jesus, we find him leading his sheep to green pastures, and streams of living water as can be seen in Psalm 23. When we explored the encounter of Jesus with the woman at the well in John 4:5-30, we saw that he spoke of offering her living water which would quench her thirst forever, welling up to eternal life. Indeed, to drink of such water would mean that she would never be thirsty again.

What then does all of this mean for us today? In a world obsessed with occupying our minds with every kind of trivial information we must learn how to listen, effectively, to Jesus. We must never forget that he offers us not only the words of life but eternal truths. Hence, we need to rediscover how to be sensitive to what Jesus is saying to us, whilst at the same time receiving it as being fresh, and life-giving, Good News. Going back to Jesus we need to recall that we are his sheep, and listen attentively to his voice, recalling that it is not one amongst many but THE WORD. This is why the image of life-giving water is so vital because without it we cannot live. Hence, we need to see such an eternal spring, as the words of Jesus surely are, as providing all that we need to stay close to him.

Having said that, Jesus also makes something else abundantly clear. It is not enough simply to listen to his voice, but we must follow him. What does this mean? Well perhaps it might help to think like this. Can we believe what Jesus believed? Can we align ourselves with those things Jesus sided with? Can we, like him, stand up for and speak for the voiceless, the weak and the vulnerable? Can we be on the side of people in need? Can we make present his mercy, compassion, forgiveness, and love? Can we, like Jesus, have complete trust in the Father? Can we, ultimately, face anything, including death, with the hope, and certainty with which he faced it?

Listening to Jesus brings us back to him and helps us reorientate our lives in the face of the daily bombardment we are all assaulted with through the mass media. When the words of Jesus are at the heart of our faith, and the communities to which we belong, something happens, transformed existence. Our lives, and the way in which we live are changed because they conform to that of Christ. When that happens others will know that they have people to turn to, and places to go, when everyone, and everything else, appears to reject them.

Something to think about and discuss:

1. *Spend some time reflecting on how much you listen to the words of Jesus.*
2. *How important are the words of Jesus to our own lives of faith, and the communities to which we belong?*
3. *Think about the sheep and the shepherd and reflect on the importance of this image to Jesus and his followers today.*
4. *In what ways would you like the church to offer more opportunities when it comes to understanding the scriptures?*
5. *Read again the final two paragraphs of this reflection. How much of it do you find yourself agreeing and disagreeing with?*

Eleven:

Love is his way

John 13:31-35

Fifth Sunday of Easter

When he had gone out, Jesus said, "Now the Son of Man has been glorified, and God has been glorified in him. If God has been glorified in him, God will also glorify him in himself and will glorify him at once. Little children, I am with you only a little longer. You will look for me; and as I said to the Jews so now, I say to you, 'Where I am going, you cannot come.' I give you a new commandment, that you love one another. Just as I have loved you, you also should love one another. By this everyone will know that you are my disciples, if you have love for one another."

Have you ever come across the word reciprocity? It means I will do something for you on the basis that, in return, you will do something for me. As such, it forms the structure for the commercial world. A number of years ago a book came out called *'The Giving Tree,'* by *Shel Silverstein (Particular Books; First Illustrated Edition (2 Dec. 2010).* Essentially the book tells the story of a boy's relationship with a tree as he goes through life. It is the tree, however, which continues to give throughout its life, whilst the boy, as he grows into manhood, only takes. As a result, some people criticised the book because of its lack of reciprocity. What I want to do now, is to use this story, as way of understanding today's Gospel reading.

We begin with Jesus showing us how he knows, full well, the vulnerability of his disciples as he prepares to leave them. For this reason, he speaks to them in words of gentle, and loving tenderness, *'My children I will be with you only a little longer.'* What are they to do without him? What will become of them? How will they survive without his constant presence? For this reason, Jesus gives them a gift to support, and encourage them when he has gone, *'A new commandment I give you. Love one another as I have loved you.'* Putting it another way, if the disciples love each other in the same way Jesus has loved them, then he will always be with them.

The nature of the love Jesus has shared with them will spread naturally amongst his disciples. It is for this very reason then, that Jesus can say, *'By this all men will know that you are my disciples, if you love one another.'*

This now becomes the true test of Christian authenticity when it comes to communities which profess their belief in him. As the love which flows from the heart of Jesus enters the lives of those who walk in his footsteps, such love defines the identity of his followers. Yet, we live in a world defined by reciprocity where, as they say, money rules all. Where does unconditional love fit into this model? How does a culture of love fit into a culture of commercial gain, even if both parties benefit from it? Indeed, what profit is there in one-sided, self-sacrificial, and unconditional love? Perhaps, the most important point to make here is that Christianity must not compromise the command of Jesus to love without personal gain. Even when this involves standing up to and resisting the prevailing culture of reciprocity. This is one of the reasons why the book I mentioned earlier, *'The Giving Tree,'* received so much criticism, at the time, because it simply went against the prevailing culture. Putting it simply, Christians inspired by Jesus, and his command to love, must resist the temptation to self-service, especially when it comes to people's lives.

Every so often we need to spend time reflecting on the command of Jesus to love others as he loves us and ask ourselves what this actually means. This needs to be done as individuals, and just as importantly, by the communities to which we belong. Remembering that such love defines who we are. This is what makes Christian communities different, by the love they have for one another. Such love needs to be reflected in our attitudes, the way in which we think, act, and treat others; even those who are not members of our communities. Love like this is radical, unconditional, and therefore challenges reciprocity at every level. Let us never forget, that all of this is based on what Jesus said, did and promised. Therefore, we must follow his example whereby he placed himself at the service of people who were very often demonised and dehumanised by their own religious leaders. This is and cannot be our way. *'A new command I give you: Love one another. As I have loved you, so must you love one another. By this all men will know that you are my disciples if you love one another.'* Love was the way of Jesus; it must be our way too.

Something to think about and discuss:

1. *See if you can find a copy of 'The Giving Tree,' and read it for yourself. Make up your own mind on what you think it might be really saying.*
2. *What are your own thoughts on reciprocity? Does it, very often, dominate our way of life today? Are there any dangers in this?*
3. *Reflect on the command of Jesus to love others as he loves us. What demands does this make on us today?*
4. *How can we recreate communities of love based on the teaching of Jesus? What ideas do you have about this for your parish?*
5. *How hard is it to live life differently, and according to the values of the kingdom of heaven, in the modern world?*

Twelve:

Filled With the Spirit

John 14:23-29

Sixth Sunday of Easter

Jesus answered him, "Those who love me will keep my word, and my Father will love them, and we will come to them and make our home with them. Whoever does not love me does not keep my words; and the word that you hear is not mine but is from the Father who sent me.

"I have said these things to you while I am still with you. But the Advocate, the Holy Spirit, whom the Father will send in my name, will teach you everything, and remind you of all that I have said to you. Peace, I leave with you; my peace I give to you. I do not give to you as the world gives. Do not let your hearts be troubled, and do not let them be afraid. You heard me say to you, 'I am going away, and I am coming to you.' If you loved me, you would rejoice that I am going to the Father, because the Father is greater than I. And now I have told you this before it occurs, so that when it does occur, you may believe."

In the Gospel of John, special place is given to what is often referred to as the farewell discourse of Jesus, whereby he prepares his disciples for when he will no longer be, physically, with them. Jesus knows, all too well, that they are afraid at the thought of his absence from them. So, he seeks to reassure them. In doing so, he makes a promise to them, the church, and in turn us, that although he has to leave them, they will, in fact, never experience his absence.

A careful reading of today's Gospel sees Jesus telling his disciples, no less than five times, that they can rely on the Holy Spirit to reassure them of his constant presence. Indeed, it is the Holy Spirit who will take care of them, providing the strength they will need, to carry-out the mission he will entrust to them. As such, therefore, the Holy Spirit will be nothing less than the living presence of Jesus in their midst. It is for this reason that Jesus can say to them, *'The Holy Spirit, whom the Father will send in my name, will teach you all things and will remind you of everything I have said to you.'*

In this way, Jesus creates what might be called a vision for the future, as to what will happen, once he has returned to the Father. Filled with the Holy Spirit his follows will set out on a mission to transform the world. Every step they take the Holy Spirit will be with them filling their minds, and hearts with the teachings of Jesus. Hence, although they will face many challenges along the way, Jesus will be always with them, and so they have nothing to fear. Yet, there is also something more, which is immensely powerful. In receiving the Spirit, the Church will take on the identity of Jesus, which in turn is also firmly rooted in the Father. It is for this reason that all those who belong to the Church represent, in a unique way, the Father and the Son. Now imagine that each of us by virtue of our baptism, and membership of the body of Christ on earth, the Church, reflect because of the indwelling of the Holy Spirit, within us, the nature, and the being of the Father and the Son.

Yet, Jesus also goes on to make clear something else clear. In giving his Spirit, he also gives his peace, *'Peace, I leave you; my peace I give you.'* Note, he does not wish them peace but rather gives them the gift of his peace. Once again, this serves to remind us that each of us constantly rests in the peace of Jesus, something we can experience every day of our lives. This, however, is a peace that the world cannot give because its source is the Spirit of truth, and should not, therefore, be confused with anything else. Hence, when the storm clouds gather, and our faith is threatened by everything which the world can throw at us. We can turn in confidence, once again, to the words of Jesus, *'Do not let your hearts be troubled and do not be afraid.'*

The peace of Christ then needs to live constantly in our hearts. For this reason, we have nothing to fear. This only happens, however, when our faith is built on the rock of the Holy Spirit which dwells within us. It is when we forget this that we become lost. As a result, we need to ask ourselves a simple question, *'Where can our true security be found?'* The answer of course, is only in

Christ. To truly be the Church, and represent the Father and the Son, we must never, therefore, give in to resentment or fear. The truth, as Jesus tells us in the Gospel reading for today, can only be found in the Spirit. It was this same Spirit which guided Jesus throughout his ministry, and it is this same Spirit which we must rely on, and be inspired by, if we are to truly reflect the nature, and the being of the Father and the Son.

Something to think about and discuss:

1. *For a moment or two reflect on your own fears. What might this tell you?*
2. *Now reflect on the constant presence of the Holy Spirit within you. How does this make you feel?*
3. *Spend some time, quietly, thinking about how your life of faith is a reflection of the presence of the Father and Son in the world.*
4. *How does your life of faith represent the peace of Christ, given to you by him, as a free gift?*
5. *'Where can our true security be found?' How would you answer this question?*

Thirteen:

What Do We Do Now?

Luke 24:46-53

The Ascension of the Lord

Then he led them out as far as Bethany, and, lifting up his hands, he blessed them. While he was blessing them, he withdrew from them and was carried up into heaven. And they worshiped him and returned to Jerusalem with great joy; and they were continually in the temple blessing God.

We are almost there and our journey through Lent and Easter, together, is nearly over. Today, we need to explore how our early brothers and sisters, in faith, continued the mission given to them by Jesus without him being physically with them. In doing this, we can also reflect on how we can develop, and maintain a relationship with Jesus without him being physically present on earth.

I have always found it interesting to note that we find no account of the Ascension of Jesus in the Gospel of Matthew. Instead, Jesus gathers his disciples together in a familiar place to them all, a mountain in Galilee. It is here that he assures them that he will, in fact, always be with them when he says, *'I am with you always to the very end of the age.'* But what does this mean, and how is it possible?

In the Gospel reading for today from Luke we find a completely different setting. Here Jesus, we are told, leaves his disciples. So, at this point, separation from him, for them, becomes a reality. Luke puts it like this, *'while he was blessing them, he left them and was taken up into heaven.'* This, therefore, is something that they, and in turn us, must accept. Yet, there is also something quite unique here, in so far as, Jesus imparts on them, his blessing. Imagine that, directly receiving the blessing of Jesus. That same blessing which he gave, throughout his earthly ministry, to all those who came to him in need.

In the Gospel of John, we have another completely different account of what happened when Jesus left his disciples. Firstly, he is aware that they are sad at the thought of him leaving them. So, he seeks to reassure them with these words, *'It is for your good that I am going away. Unless I go away, the Counsellor will not come to you; but if I go, I will send him to you.'* What then is going on here? What is Jesus telling his disciples, the church and in turn us today? Perhaps, Jesus wants them, to stand on their own two feet, and accept the responsibility he is giving to them to carry-out his mission. This, in fact, is the mark of a good teacher. Good teachers do not do everything for you. Rather, they equip you with the right skills to do things for yourself.

Jesus promises his disciples that he will send them the gift of the Holy Spirit, and therefore will be with them for all time. It is through the grace of the Holy Spirit that they will grow in faith, and understanding of the mission which Jesus has entrusted to them. Hence, they must not stand still but grow, and accept the responsibility he has given to them. Think back to what Jesus said in his parables about seeds and growth. Do not be afraid to grow in your faith, to be ever creative, and see things in a new way. Hence, we are called to engage with the culture of the day, and not withdraw from it because what we have is Good News, and it is meant to be shared.

All this serves to remind us that we are the church, the body of Christ on earth, filled with his life-giving Spirit. It is through the Spirit that we are called to grow, knowing, and believing that we are strengthened, upheld, and sustained by the constant presence of Jesus, without whom we can do nothing. It is for this reason that we should never be afraid of exploring new, and creative ways to teach, preach and bear witness to the Gospel of truth. This is the age of the Holy Spirit, poured out constantly into our hearts, driving the church and its people, ever forward. It is for this reason that the mission of the church can never fail. And what is that mission, you may well ask? To make Christ known.

Something to think about and discuss:

1. *What does the Ascension of Jesus mean to you?*
2. *Why do you think the Gospels have different ways of expressing the physical absence of Jesus?*
3. *Spend some time reflecting on the blessing of Jesus described in Luke. What does this mean for you?*
4. *Think about how the Good News of Jesus Christ might be presented in a new way to the people of today.*
5. *What does it mean to be living in the age of the Spirit? How might this effect the role of the church and our lives of faith?*

Fourteen:

All things are possible

John 14:15-16, 23-26

Pentecost Sunday

Jesus said to his disciples:

'If you love me, you will keep my commandments. And I will ask the Father, and he will give you another Advocate, to be with you forever.

Jesus answered him, "Those who love me will keep my word, and my Father will love them, and we will come to them and make our home with them. Whoever does not love me does not keep my words; and the word that you hear is not mine but is from the Father who sent me.

"I have said these things to you while I am still with you. But the Advocate, the Holy Spirit, whom the Father will send in my name, will teach you everything, and remind you of all that I have said to you."

*

'Where is God?' 'How can God be everywhere at the same time?' 'Why can't we see God?' 'Why doesn't God show himself?' 'Can God do anything?' 'Who made God?' 'Does God know everything?' 'Where is heaven?' 'Will heaven ever get full up?'

These are just some of the questions I am asked by children when I summon up enough courage to go into a school. Indeed, it was for this reason that I wrote the book, *'Only in the Crucified God – Questions and answers on faith, hope and love.'* Here, I am not going to answer all of them now, but as we move from the Ascension to Pentecost, I will attempt to tackle some of them. The first point I would make, however, is this. The incarnation of Jesus, the fact that God became human, is only complete when Jesus ascends to his Father, taking with him our humanity. It is worthwhile thinking about the implications of this for a moment or two. Our humanity, through Jesus, is now with God. Therefore, he knows because he experienced, directly through his Son, everything we go through in life. Thus, there is no sphere of human life, which is alien to God. I do not know where you are in life, at the moment, or what you are going through, but our faith tells us that God does.

Now let me go back to the Ascension of Jesus. To say Jesus has returned to the Father is the same as saying to a child, he has, in fact, gone back to heaven. This, of course, is true. However, does this mean that he has abandoned us though? The above paragraph dismisses such a notion. But how is intimacy with Jesus maintained if he is no longer physically present on earth? What I am going to say now, in response to this question, might sound a little complex, but I will attempt to explain it in such a way that I hope you will find it accessible.

To say Jesus has gone to heaven is to attempt to explain how he has moved into a different way of existing, which does not mean he has gone to another place. Rather, that he now lives beyond the time and space that we know, and experience. In this way he can, in fact, be present everywhere, at the same time, because he is not limited to existing in the time and space that we know. Accordingly, in his earthly ministry, Jesus purposefully limited himself to existing in our time and space. The resurrected Jesus, however, had been transformed. One minute he was with his disciples, and in the blink of an eye he was gone. The Jesus of the Ascension can, however, now be intimately present with us for all time. Hence, we can say, he is never absent but always present. Remember the words of Jesus to Thomas, *'more blessed are those who cannot see and yet still believe.'* For this reason, we are more blessed than the disciples of Jesus because, in truth, Jesus is constantly with us.

Today, we celebrate the outpouring of the Holy Spirit as Father and Son are reunited. Their unconditional love for each other now overspills into us, so that we become energised by their grace. Hence, there now dwells within each, and every single one of us, the life-giving Spirit of Jesus. We are tasked now, as we said in an earlier reflection, to listen only to Jesus. To allow his voice, and his words to penetrate the depths of our heart and soul. In this way, the Holy Spirit summons us, wherever we go and whatever we do, to bear witness to Jesus. Knowing, and believing that Jesus is with us always, we can now like him, call God Our Father, and treat each other as brothers and sisters. Guided and driven by the Holy Spirit we can now work together, as the people of God, to build his Kingdom of mercy, compassion, forgiveness, and love. In all things we are commissioned to conform our lives to that of Christ. Now we must, therefore, speak out on behalf of the voiceless, seek out and serve the poor and the needy, welcome the stranger, and always be willing to be on the side of the rejected, despised, unwanted, and unloved. However, this is only possible when we open our minds, hearts, and souls to the indwelling of the Holy Spirit, and when we do that, all things are possible.

Something to think about and discuss:

1. *Look at the questions at the beginning of this reflection. How would you answer them?*
2. *How is it possible for us to be closer to Jesus now than his disciples were over 2,000 years ago?*
3. *Reflect on how it is possible for Jesus to be present everywhere at the same time.*
4. *How important is the Holy Spirit to your life of faith?*
5. *What might the Holy Spirit be calling you to do now?*

Some Final Thoughts

I started this book by saying, in the introduction, that this would be my last writing project based exclusively on the Bible. In that sense, I have not changed my mind but there is one more task I have set myself, which is to write a personal reflection on the relationship between faith and mental health. I will say more about that another time, but for now, if you have been part of my journey so far, there is, at least, one more adventure for us to share together, sometime in the future.

As I complete this project, however, I would like to say one or two things about the nature of vocation, which is something, I believe, we are all called to. Indeed, it is only because of my own vocation as a deacon, in the catholic church, that I have been able to write any of the books listed, at the end, of this one.

The essence of a vocation, to me at least, is that it is personal. It comes from something deep within your soul, finding expression in the best of yourself. For this reason, and inevitably, a vocation is all about what you are good at. It is because of this that a vocation draws upon every aspect of your life – physical, mental, emotional, and spiritual. So, in a very real sense, it is about how you live your life day in and day out. As a result, there can be no real separation between your vocation and how you live your life. Here, I am not talking, exclusively, about a religious vocation but any walk of life, and any kind of work. However, I would always link it to the common good. In the same way, a true vocation is never at variance with your conscience and is always a force for good in the world. It is also important to understand that at the heart of every vocation is sheer joy.

When we follow our vocation there may have to be, and once again inevitably, sacrifice. But we do so willingly. It is for this reason, that we may have to put wealth to one side though there may always be the need to support our families and loved ones. Yet, the joy we find in our vocation is part of what we can offer to others and the world. It is for this reason that generosity is also an essential part of any vocation. We are called, in effect, to share the joy, we find in what we do, with others. This is because at the heart of a vocation is the well-spring of living water, welling up within us, an inner source of power, if you like, which ultimately leads to the living of a fulfilled life. Hence, it is my belief that we all have a vocation because we are all made in the image of God. Oscar Romero once said, something along the lines of, that the vocation of the Christian is to defend the image of God in all people. When we see all our fellow human beings like that our perception of the world changes. This is especially true when, and where, anyone is prevented from following their own vocation. When this happens, we have a responsibility to make sure that we have done everything we possibly can to live out, to the best of our ability, what Christ has called us to do.

This book has been my attempt to help you, the reader, find Christ in the Sunday Gospels of Lent and Easter. In this way, all of us can begin to understand the nearness of God, and his great desire that, through the life, death, and resurrection of his Son, we may not only know him but fall in love with him. There have been challenges, quite rightly, along the way but in the words of Saint Paul in his letter to the Romans, *'Nothing can separate us from the love of God revealed in Christ Jesus, Our Lord.'* If, therefore, we are to respond to his invitation to follow him, and in so doing discover our own vocation, then it must be as a response to his love for us. You see, once we discover that we are loved, unconditionally by God, everything we do must then be interpreted in the light of that love. Hence, no vocation is any more or any less important than any other because everything we do is for the glory of God.

Sometimes, there can appear to be, this huge gap between what we believe we are called to do, and what we actually can do. This is something that we just have to learn to accept. Yet, it is also something that we must never deny. You see to deny our true vocation is ultimately to deny our true selves, and as I have found, personally, it is always something which will return time, and time again. Everything I have written in this closing part of the book is aimed at encouraging you, the reader, to continue to explore what Christ might be inviting you to do. Over the years I have discovered that my own vocation is an expression of who I really aim. There is no difference to be found in what I do, and who I am, because the two are completely one. I call this wholeness or oneness in Christ. It is for this reason that every word, in every book, I have ever written, is nothing less than an expression of my own faith in Christ, who called me to be his servant in the world. There is great joy in this for me and generosity too. I have had the privilege of being inspired by the Grace of the Holy Spirit to write a series of books whose primary aim is to help others deepen their faith in Christ. At the same time, and where I have been allowed, the profits from the sales of these books have been donated to charities helping some of the poorest and most wretched people on earth. This I hope, and I pray, is a true reflection of who I am, nothing less than a humble and obedient servant of Christ, who came himself not to be served but to serve. I thank you for joining me for part of the journey, but it is now time for us to go our separate ways. Pray for me as I will for you, and never forget that Christ is closer to you than you could ever imagine and loves you more than you could ever know.

God Bless.

Deacon Sean

Thank You

This book has been a long time in the writing. It has, in fact, taken me a lifetime, though, if truth be told, I was never really aware of it. Looking back now I can appreciate that there were moments in my life when Christ spoke to me through the love of others, and for this reason, I would like to pay tribute to them here as I write my last few words. Some of them have left this world, whilst most will never even know I have written this book. Yet, that does not seem to matter now. What is far more important to me, however, is that I remember them, and am grateful for those moments, through the grace of God, when our lives coincided. So, I begin with a thank you to my family. To my wife, Pam, and my three sons, Lance, Thomas, and James. Then there's my parents Bridie and Joe and my sister Kate. At this point, I must also pay tribute to the people and nation of Ireland where, thanks to my grandmother, my faith was originally born. Over the years, there have many teachers who have taken me under their wing and inspired me. One, however, stands out because I owe him so much. His name is John Jarvis, and he believed in me when no one else did by pushing the right buttons at the right time, to get me over the line. John, I owe you more than words can say. I also thank the people, parish, clergy, and school of Our Lady of the Wayside where I have spent the whole of my ministry as a deacon. The best place to learn anything about God is with people because that is where he is to be found. It is also important for me to thank you, the reader, for joining me along the way. As I said, earlier in this book, it is impossible for the author not to reveal something of themselves in the words they write. Perhaps, then, you know me a little better now. There is always a chance, however, in writing a 'thank you' that you leave someone out, albeit unintentionally. It is for this reason that I would like to thank everyone I have ever met for giving me the opportunity to encounter Christ in a variety of unique ways. Finally, and most importantly, it is only right that I thank Our

Lord for not only journeying with me but for inspiring and sustaining me along the way. There have been many times when I have been tempted to give up but there has been one thing which has kept me going, and that can be found on the dedication page of this book but just to remind you here they are again, *'for without me you can do nothing.'* How true is that!

God Bless.

Deacon Sean

About the Author

Sean Loone is a Roman Catholic Deacon working in the Archdiocese of Birmingham. He has spent much of his career teaching in a variety of schools and colleges combining this with lecturing part-time at Saint Mary's College Oscott, the seminary for the Archdiocese. Currently he acts as chaplain and Religious Education advisor to a number of academic establishments including Our Lady of the Wayside, his home parish, where he is also the Catholic Life governor. His academic interests, on which he has published many articles, include Biblical studies and Christology. His most recent publication was a book called, **'When Love Came Down – Finding Christ in the Sunday Gospels of Advent and Christmas.'** He also has extensive pastoral and sacramental experience combining this with a ministry dedicated to proclaiming God's word through both preaching and teaching the scriptures. He is married with three sons, and is currently working on his final project, which aims, this time, to explore the relationship between faith and mental health.

By the Same Author

'Born for Us
– A Journey into the Real Meaning of Christmas'
Available from ALIVE Publishing (2019)

'Only in the Crucified Christ
– Questions and Answers on Faith, Hope and Love'
Available from Amazon (2020)
All profits to CAFOD

'Sharing in the Life of God
– A Journey into the Real Meaning of Easter'
Available from Amazon (2021)
All profits to the Father O'Mahony Memorial Trust

'Servants of the Word
– The Gospel of Christ and the Call to Discipleship'
Available from Amazon (2021)
All profits to Father Hudson's Care

'Words of Life
– The Parables of Jesus for People Today'
Michael Terence Publishing (2022)
All Profits to CAFOD

'When Love Came Down
– Finding Christ in the Sunday Gospels of Advent and Christmas'
Michael Terence Publishing (2023)
All Profits to The SVP
(Our Lady of the Wayside Catholic Church)

Postscript

Having finished the book, a thought came to me, which I felt compelled to write about, and this seemed to be the best place to do it. As you can imagine, over the years, I have received feedback on the various writing projects I have embarked upon. Some of these comments have been positive whilst others have not. That I might say is perfectly normal. Yet from time-to-time others have told me, if God loves all people unconditionally, why bother becoming a Christian or indeed a Catholic at all? My instinctive reaction to this is to invite people to go and read the Gospels. After all, with whom did Jesus spend the vast majority of his time? The answer, of course, is with the prostitutes, tax collectors and sinners. The very people the religious leaders of the day identified as being condemned by God. What does that tell you? Then there is Jesus's choice of disciples, Judas would betray him, Peter denies ever having known him and Matthew was, as you may well know, a tax collector. Then there are the words of Saint Paul in his letter to the Romans, *'I am convinced of this, that nothing can ever come between us, and the love of God revealed in Christ Jesus Our Lord.'* You see, once you fall in love with Christ all you want to do is to tell others about him, not so much by what you say but how you live. Personally, I never grow tired of referring to the Father as the God of mercy, compassion, forgiveness, and love. Then there are all those people, all over the world, who through no fault of their own, have never *known* God. What about them? I can say this because I was once one of them myself, and if we are not careful, even though we may call ourselves Christian, we may in truth not really know the God revealed by Jesus Christ at all.

A careful reading of the Hebrew scriptures (The Old Testament) reveals the mission of Israel, as the people of God, to be nothing less than *'a light to the nations.'* (Isaiah 42:6) Or putting it another way, their faith is meant to draw all people to the Father. At the Second Vatican Council the Church was identified to be, *Lumen*

Gentium, a light to the nations. That is, to proclaim the Gospel of Jesus Christ, for all people. Many of the parables, which Jesus uses to teach about the nature and being of God, reveal this truth. Think about the *Tenants In the Vineyard*, where all the workers are paid the same wage, irrespective of the amount of time they spend working. Then there is the *Good Samaritan*, where it is the foreigner who reveals the compassion of God. Finally, spend any time with the parable of the *Lost Son*, and you will begin to grasp what the mercy, forgiveness, and love of God is really like.

The Catholic writer J. R. R. Tolkien made something very clear in two great characters he created, Bilbo Baggins in *The Hobbit*, and Frodo in *The Lord of the Rings*. That experience shapes who we become, or that we are the sum total of our experiences, if we have the courage to embrace and accept them. It is for this reason that I have become, over the years, a firm believer in the *theology of experience*. That is, we meet and encounter God in our own experiences of life. Whether they be good or bad, the highs and the lows, even in the depths of hopelessness and despair, God is always present and never absent. Look at how Matthew begins his Gospel, *'and they shall call his name Emmanuel, which means God- is-with-us.'* Now look at how he ends his Gospel, *'I am with you always, till the end of time.'* After all, this is the true meaning of the incarnation, our belief that in and through His Son, God became one of us. Even the great church father Irenaeus was able to proclaim that God became human so that we could share in his divinity. Hence, I am absolutely convinced that in and through the life, death and resurrection of His Son, Jesus Christ, God does in fact, love all people unconditionally. I have learnt this not from any book but from my own brutal experiences of life. It is for this reason, that I am able to say time and time again that *God is closer to us than we could ever imagine and loves us more than we could ever know.* That is the Gospel, or the Good news of Jesus Christ, and my own experiences have taught me, that it is in fact, written on my heart, as it is on yours too.

Finally, reflect back on the story of Lazarus (John 11:1-44), it is well worth another read. He lies dead, buried in the tomb, wrapped in his burial shroud, and Jesus calls him forth in the words, '*Lazarus, come out.*' Now think about what Jesus said In John 10:10, '*I have come that you may have life.*' At this point stop and apply these words to yourself and your own life. No matter where you are or what you have gone through or what is happening to you now. Whether you have been a Christian all your life, some of it or indeed for none of it, simply hear these words spoken directly to you and your own heart, '*I have come that you may have life.*' You see God desires that we are not meant to stay in the darkness of the tomb, symbolising all the pain, misery and suffering we endure. Rather, the crucified God invites us to put our hand into his, and with him walk out of the darkness and into the light because it is in that moment, we undergo our own resurrection and Easter lives in us.

'I am the resurrection and the life. Anyone who believes in me, even though that person dies, will live, and no one who lives and believes in me will ever die.'

(John 11:25-26)

'I have come so that they may have life and have it in plenty.'

(John 10:10)

'The light shines in the darkness and the darkness cannot overcome it.'

(John 1:5)

'And look, I am with you always till the end of time.'

(Matthew 28:20)

'For I am convinced that neither life nor death, nor angels, nor rulers, nothing already in existence and nothing still to come, nor any power, nor height nor depths, nor any created thing will be able to separate us from the love of God in Christ Jesus Our Lord.'

Romans (8:37-39)

'Anyone who gives so much as a cup of cold water.'

(Matthew 10:42)

Available worldwide from Amazon

www.mtp.agency

www.facebook.com/mtp.agency

@mtp_agency

Printed in Great Britain
by Amazon

37333251R00101